Sex Ed
for
Caring Schools

Sex Ed
for
Caring Schools

CREATING AN ETHICS-BASED CURRICULUM

SHARON LAMB

Teachers College, Columbia University
New York and London

Published by Teachers College Press, 1234 Amsterdam Avenue, New York, NY 10027

Library of Congress Cataloging-in-Publication Data

Lamb, Sharon.
  Sex ed for caring schools : creating an ethics-based curriculum / Sharon Lamb.
    p. cm.
  Includes bibliographical references and index.
  ISBN 978-0-8077-5398-9 (pbk. : alk. paper) — ISBN 978-0-8077-5399-6 (hardcover : alk. paper)
    1. Sex instruction—Curricula—United States. 2. Sexual ethics—Study and teaching—United States. I. Title. II. Title: Sex education for caring schools.
  HQ57.5.A3L36 2013
  372.37′2—dc23   2012043139

ISBN 978-0-8077-5398-9 (paperback)
ISBN 978-0-8077-5399-6 (hardcover)

Printed on acid-free paper
Manufactured in the United States of America

20 19 18 17 16 15 14 13   8 7 6 5 4 3 2 1

Contents

Acknowledgments

I want to thank the people who have helped me to write this book and especially the curriculum that goes with it. I have a cadre of brilliant students with whom I have been privileged to work. Aleksandra Plocha has been my right-hand woman this year, organizing me and my thoughts and offering smart critiques and wise thoughts of her own. Kara Lustig and Kelly Graling have also been my partners in crime as we've waded through a dozen or more curricula. Kara and Kelly joined me in a deep critique of current curricula, sorting through quotes and developing themes that are presented in two published papers (Lamb, Graling, & Lustig, 2011; Lamb, Lustig, & Graling, in press). Their influence is present in a number of sections on the Sexual Ethics for a Caring Society curricular materials. Many students wrote portions of the material that forms the basis of much of Chapters 5 and 6, and I attempt to acknowledge the students who made primary contributions through footnotes. Know, however, that in group collaborations, many of the lessons were written collaboratively. These contributors are Aleksandra Plocha, Kara Lustig, Kelly Graling, Paula Moebus, Shin-Ye Kim, Kathryn Hall, and Judea Beatrice. These students not only informed my thinking through their work on the curriculum but are co-authors of the online curriculum. Kaelin Farmer wrote many of the discussion questions that appear in Appendix A, delightfully engaging with the material and imagining herself an undergrad again. Kaelin and Kimberly Parker lovingly attended to the writing and the references in their typically thorough ways. I am grateful for Kimberly's training in Latin and Classics. The curriculum itself also contains work by Bettina Love that has been summarized in the section on hip hop music.

At the beginning of my work, the teaching of Michael Sandel in his Harvard course on ethics, a course I took 20 years ago and retook online recently, was very influential (Sandel, 2011). I also depended on presentations a Carnegie Mellon professor, Robert Cavalier, put online for everyone's use (Cavalier, 2011). He inspired me to put my own curriculum online and to make it available at no cost. I want to acknowledge the kind and helpful conversations I had on this topic with philosophers

Alan Wertheimer, Jeffrie Murphy, and Alan Soble, all of whom I greatly admire. My thinking on this topic was enhanced by Dennis Carlson and Donelle Roseboro, who brought scholars together for a conference sponsored by the Ford Foundation. I also want to thank Mary Lou Rasmussen and Daniel Marshall, who brought together sex education critics and authors from around the world to a conference in the summer of 2011 (in Italy, no less) to discuss sex education. Saint Michael's College provided me with funding early on to buy curricula and support this work. The fantastic Sexuality Information and Education Council of the United States (SIECUS), with Monica Rodriguez and Max Cardullo, leant me curricula they had in their library. Bill Taverner of New Jersey Planned Parenthood has been extremely helpful in getting me information and materials I need. The Association for Moral Education (AME) gave me a Mid-Career Sabbatical Grant to write the curriculum, and this funding came from the Lisa Kuhmerker Gift of Time to AME. The University of Massachusetts in Boston has also generously supported this work with start-up funds, travel money, and research support. And I appreciate the editors at the *Harvard Educational Review* who, when they sent back my first manuscript, told me I had written enough for a small book!

I have to thank my friends on the sidelines, ready to cheer me on when I feel defeated or not quite smart enough for a task, particularly Lyn Mikel Brown, who always knows the right thing to say. One friend, philosopher Larry Blum, has consistently encouraged my forays into the field of ethics and has helped me to nuance my philosophical thinking when I share it with him, just as Jeanne Marecek helps me to nuance my feminist psychology writing. Jan Steutel, Doret de Ruyter, and the late Ben Spiecker provided many good conversations about sex education at AME conferences, and their own writing has been influential. And, finally, I appreciate the time that my family members, Paul, Willy, and Julian, have dedicated to reading parts of this work. I was glad to have their editorial opinions, and frankly, in the case of Julian, I was glad to give him a little sex ed in addition to the paltry information he received as a student.

INTRODUCTION

Sex Ed with Character, Citizenship, and Caring

Who actually teaches sex ed today in the classroom? Health teachers? Yes. In more liberal school districts health teachers can warn students against sexually transmitted infections (STIs) and pregnancy and provide valuable health information. Gym teachers? Yes. But do we ever ask ourselves why gym teachers are given this role? Is sex a sport? Do principals believe they know the body better than other teachers? Do we automatically turn to them as a source of information for all things physical? Or are they simply the teachers who have some spare time available in order to fill a niche or advisory period in the schedule? What about other teachers in the school, those who attend training courses to learn how to teach Abstinence Only Until Marriage (AOUM) curricula only to return to school fully armed with slogans and horror stories about regrettable sex? They teach sex ed, too. And what about trained personnel from outside of the school from organizations like Planned Parenthood, or from rape awareness or peer education programs, who are invited to hold one, two, or maybe three classes on valuable information such as contraception use? They too teach sex ed.

But the best answer to the question of who will teach sex ed is, *you,* the reader. Teachers in training to teach a variety of content courses—history, English, social studies, and other topics—can teach sex ed in middle schools and high schools because sex ed needs to be about more than health. And the teaching of sex ed is part of a larger critical pedagogy project that asks students to learn to critique education and the oppressive aspects of institutions that affect the way they live. *Sex Ed for Caring Schools* presents the background and framework of a curriculum that goes beyond the typical health curriculum students receive today. It advocates for a curriculum that helps students develop awareness and understand the complexity of what it means to be a sexual person in today's world. As part of a critical pedagogy movement that connects education to social justice enterprises, this book and the corresponding online curriculum encourage students to see themselves as sexual citizens and to talk, write,

1

and think about the moral issues underlying so much of sex. Those of you who have engaged in critical pedagogy in your classes today or who are inspired by the teachings of Freire and his successors, who discuss how postmodern, feminist, anti-racist, and queer theories impact education today, are in a unique position to advocate for a comprehensive and morality-based sex ed course. Even if a school lacks adequate time to present the full course, this book, with its emphasis on ethical issues involved in sex for youths, is relevant to you, given your unique opportunity to educate, provoke discussion, and nudge students to be ethically minded thinkers and actors in the sexual world they live in. Those of you training to be middle school or high school teachers of English, social studies, and other subjects can take initiative and volunteer to teach such a course or incorporate moral discussions into your classes.

Even though sex education in the United States today takes place in a post-Pill and post-*Roe v. Wade* era; even though it is being taught to students, the majority of whom will be having some kind of sex in high school; even though students today see pornography fairly regularly, watch TV shows in which there are frank and humorous discussions about sex, and can go on several websites to get information about the most typical to the most unusual sexual practices, sex education now is, for many students, an irrelevant course—for some even damaging. At its best, today's school-based sex ed provides students with health information and a space to discuss and weigh options regarding personal decisions. This kind of sex ed has been called Comprehensive Sexuality Education (CSE) and stands in contrast to Abstinence Only Until Marriage (AOUM) sex education.

The word "comprehensive" used to mean something more comprehensive than it does today, and the vestiges of curricula that are a part of that movement for an all-encompassing sex ed class can be seen online in courses such as the King County *Family Life and Sexual Health* (*FLASH*) curriculum, which is a school-based comprehensive curriculum in Seattle; in the massive curriculum by Advocates for Youth, parts of which can and are incorporated into school-based and community-based programs; and in the *Our Whole Lives* (*OWL*) curriculum, which is associated with the Unitarian Universalist Church and predominantly taught in church. These curricula are excellent, despite their shared tendency to address students in too simple a manner, directing material to the least accomplished students rather than to the average or smartest. Though comprehensive, they, like most CSE programs, use simple social-skills training exercises, role plays, and workbook-type assignments in a manner similar to the more limited school-based comprehensive curricula being practiced today. Still, these curricula, unlike their successors of the "comprehensive" variety, contain moral messages about not harming others, exercising one's rights, and respecting fellow students who may have different views.

When I began to look closely at the curricula in use today, from the pregnancy and HIV/AIDS prevention curricula to the AOUM curricula, I started to think about how we could and should do more with ethics. As a member of the Association for Moral Education (AME) and its current president, I've been interested in the development of morality for some time. In my early years, training to do Kohlberg coding of moral interviews and working with Carol Gilligan on her early moral interviews for her paradigm-changing book, *In a Different Voice*, I learned to think of morality as not something that was passed down from adults to children—what the developmental psychologist Jean Piaget called *heteronymous* morality (1948)—but as something that students develop in relation to one another, in relationships that are more or less equal. I also learned to understand moral development as different in different contexts and even dependent on the power and position one has in society—for example, girls having been brought up in a context that emphasized concern for the other and that prioritized injunctions such as "do no harm" over "preserve rights." This training taught me to question the Western emphasis on rights and justice, or at least to consider alternative moralities as ideologies potentially meaningful for youths.

As a feminist, I have been concerned for a long time about issues such as sexual harassment, sexual abuse and victimization, girls' empowerment, and coercive, narrow gender roles. I've also studied media and marketing influences on girls' and boys' conceptions of themselves and what it means to be a girl and a boy. From a postmodern perspective I have analyzed and deconstructed discourse around gender, abuse, violence, sexuality, and empowerment, ultimately extending this work to the discourses dominating sex ed curricula. This feminist perspective is tied to the perspective I bring from the field of moral education in that I desire for girls and boys to be freed from rigid gender roles and to be empowered to critically examine marketing and media stereotypes that restrict their growth and ultimately limit their potential.

As a child psychologist who treats children and adolescents in a therapy office, researches them as a scholar, and cares about their growth, I also care about sex ed in its current and inadequate state. I understand that sexual development starts at birth and that children play sexual games and have sexual experiences with one another as they gradually develop a more adult understanding of sexuality. I want deeply for them to have these experiences without shame, without being accused of sex offending, and to have the opportunity to work out their thoughts and feelings about sex in a space that permits a range of affects and questions. I also want them to know from an early age about what hurts, what respecting others entails, and that sex is as much about relationships as it is about what protects, works, or feels good.

This book, then, and the online curriculum accompanying it emerge ultimately from my own diverse educational background: moral education, feminist education, and child psychology.

Liberals today, I have noticed, do not use the "v" word much! By the "v" word I mean "values," not "vagina," a word, incidentally, liberal sex educators have very few qualms using. Values have come to be associated with conservative and Christian fundamentalist groups in the United States who want to preserve values in American families and who claim that liberals are value-less. Because of this, and because in philosophy, values and ethics are not necessarily synonymous, I use the word "ethics" in this book. I want to bring ethics back into the liberal discourse around sex education. I see the point of conservatives, who claim that sex education as it is proposed by liberals is problematic because it is value-less. I see their point that by not teaching values we are in effect telling youths that whatever they think is right—or what their parents tell them is right—must be right. And I see them struggling in their curricula to not only impart values, but to create conversations in which students discuss values with one another. I also see their point that religion should be a part of sex ed discussions and removing religion from the picture is disrespectful to the parents who want a certain kind of education for their children.

In designing this curriculum I gave weight to these concerns and started to imagine a curriculum that could not only talk about family values but talk about ethical principles. I thought about how the human motive to care for another person and character traits such as generosity, empathy, and compassion were important traits to explore with regard to sexual behavior. I also began to entertain the possibility of introducing religion into the classroom. According to my younger son, the best course he has taken was a world religion course, offered in 9th grade at a private school in Vermont and taught by a newly graduated philosophy major from Middlebury College. Now in college, he is still interested in the religions he took interest in during that course, deepening his knowledge of them. To bring religion into the classroom is not the same as teaching someone to practice a religion other than his or her own; rather, it is teaching him or her to understand difference, to hear about how sexuality is conceptualized in religions other than one's own, and even to understand the diversity in practice in one's own religion.

I am not the first nor will I be the last to say that sex ed ought to be moral ed. Many have had similar concerns coming from the right, left, and center. When I began to research the history of sex education in the United States, I was taken aback by some of the older texts. More than 100 years ago, people also interested in ethics had an interest in the sexual lives of adolescents and wrote about it. I was embarrassed to read that I shared a concern that Eugenicists wrote about back in the early 20th century, a concern that we needed to offset the education our youths were getting from the world around them; that popular culture can be damaging. Evangeline Young wrote in her introduction to March's *Towards Racial Health* (Young, 1919) that parents had failed to take notice of the

> low tone which has pervaded the literature, drama, films, and music of the past decade, and have failed to sense the social dangers accompanying the introduction of pagan forms of dancing. The business interests which sell various forms of amusement to young people know exactly how to use this material to their own best advantage. The resulting sexual ideals and habits of boys and girls in many instances are disastrous. (p. xii)

Never would I have thought I would have anything in common with someone concerned with racial "health," but I had to face the fact that this concern of Young was exactly the concern that worried Lyn Mikel Brown, Mark Tappan, and me when we wrote *Packaging Girlhood* (2007) and *Packaging Boyhood* (2009). We were worried that marketers and media today portray a version of what it means to be a sexual human being that is problematic for boys and girls and based on stereotypes. We were also concerned about the crassness in the media surrounding sex and primarily worried that, during a time of AOUM ascendancy, this was the only message available to boys and girls.

As I read on, I discovered there were others like me in history who worried not only about the representation of sex in the media but about the representation of sex in schools in a way that showed little consideration of ethics and relationships. Indeed, the more familiar I became with the history of sex education in the United States, the more I could see that I was taking contradictory sides in several arguments that have existed for over a century.

When I write, as I will later in this book, that I want ethics to return to sex education in high schools, I am one in a long line who have made that cry, from early social hygienists with whom I would have deep disagreements, to the liberals in the 1960s who wanted ethics as part of Family Life Sex Education (FLSE).

When I write that a predominantly health-focused curriculum is problematic, I have the support of several others before me who argued that sex education based on fear of disease is not enough.

When I write about the need for inclusion and gender equity, I recognize that many before me have made similar demands, even if the conceptualization of gender equity has changed significantly over time. I was surprised to find in a 1914 text the warning that girls and boys can have equally strong urges and that it is a myth that the male sex drive is overpowering. Was this a surprisingly just treatment of sexuality and gender? Or was this part of a longstanding view that sees women as lustful creatures able to tempt men from the right path, a view that was later rejected in favor of one that held women as pure and devoid of sexual appetite?

When I write about the need for student-centered learning and democratic education, I am writing in solidarity with the teachers in California in the 1970s who opened the classroom up to students to run, believing that handing over the reins to students increased responsibility and helped them to "own" their education, to use a modern phrase. This understanding is consistent with Lawrence Kohlberg's thinking about the democratic classroom experience in the "Just Schools" approach (Kohlberg, Lieberman, Higgins, & Power, 1982).

Finally, I'd like to explain why I chose to use the phrase "sex ed" instead of "sexuality education" (or "sexualities education," as it is called in Great Britain). Social constructionism, postmodernism, discourse theory, feminism, and queer theory have all brought our attention to the use and meaning of words such as "sex" and "gender" and "sexuality," as well as the playful use of demeaning words such as "queer" and "slut" in a way that reclaims them and embraces acts and identities that were formerly condemned. Because I am reverting to an older phrase, I want to acknowledge the reasons good people such as those at the Sexuality Information and Education Council of the United States (SIECUS) organized the change of wording from sex ed to sexuality education. The first is that "sex" has come to refer to what one does sexually with another person, whereas "sexuality" refers to the whole realm of events, identities, and practices having to do with sex. The second is that "sex" has come to refer to biological sex rather than gender and so use of the word "sex" evokes a feeling of biology and destiny rather than an understanding that we are talking about a social construction. Still, I am going to retain the use of "sex ed" and "sex education" for this book because the transformation of this language no longer seems necessary for a progressive agenda, because it is shorter and catchier (!), and because the kind of curriculum I am advocating is wide-ranging at the same time as it is focused on the construction of sexualities. By calling such a curriculum "sex ed," I believe I am reclaiming the meaning of it.

HOW TO USE THIS BOOK

In this book I remind readers what the word "comprehensive" for sex ed was meant to include (as opposed to the all-but-comprehensive sex education that has morphed into "evidence-based" sex ed). A comprehensive sex education includes education on character, on citizenship, and on caring—the three Cs. Concern for society also means that in sex education we can encourage students to "think big"—to think not only about whether media versions of sexuality may be harmful to them but whether or not there is a social problem with these depictions.

In the spirit of critical pedagogy, this book begins with background, moves on to critique, and then introduces the idea of how to infuse sex ed with ethics. Chapter 1 gives a brief history of sex ed and makes the case for the inclusion of ethics. Chapter 2 introduces readers to the criticisms that have been leveled at sex ed curricula—primarily AOUM curricula but also some CSE curricula—over the late 20th and early 21st centuries and investigates how character, mutuality, responsibility to self and society, and care for others are currently represented. Chapter 3 presents an in-depth exploration of the kinds of ethics sex ed curricula endorse and should endorse. Chapter 4 reviews what it means to have citizenship education, and presents guidelines for implementing and creating an ethical, democratic sex ed curriculum. Chapter 5 asks what kinds of ethics a student needs to develop for interpersonal interactions involving sex. While past curricula focused on the policing, restricting, and protecting of girls, this chapter focuses on what education both girls and boys might need to treat one another ethically. Chapter 6 moves beyond interpersonal moral acts and explores what students can learn about sex in society at large. What are they confronted with in society and how can they develop attitudes and positions that will make them better citizens? While older curricula may have focused on the self and ways for students to cope with the barrage of material from the media and elsewhere, this curriculum presupposes an engagement with the world—that is, viewing the student not as someone who passively receives bad influences, but as someone who participates and has a hand in forming social discourse through his or her own attitudes, as well as through present and future participation.

This book can be used with pre-service teachers and other graduate students in education or related fields for one or two class periods and includes discussion questions, assignments, and sample curricula lessons in the appendixes. The curriculum that this book provides the framework for has been designed to encourage ethical and democratic sexual citizenship, and is available online for use in part or in its entirety in the classroom (www.sexandethics.org). Moreover, some of the assignments in this book ask students to go to the website and post a comment or revise a lesson to update it. In bringing to life this curriculum through this book, I hope that new teachers, regardless of their specialty, will encourage their schools to undertake this important area of adolescent learning and development. Indeed, the curriculum itself, with its readings from the fields of philosophy, psychology, and sociology, could be taught as an academic elective for post-health-course students.

This book will serve three purposes for these students: (1) It introduces students to the field of sex ed; (2) as with all critical pedagogy, it provides them with an overview of critiques and asks them to take a critical stance toward some material; and (3) it presents a new view of a comprehensive sex ed curriculum that comes from a liberal arts, democratic, and ethical perspective. This kind of curriculum is not meant to take the place of a health curriculum. Access to health information is currently the cause that rallies progressives. I have little to add to this discussion except to say that as a matter of course, health information must be provided to students; it is our ethical responsibility to give good health information to teens regarding contraception and STIs. It is also important to note that this curriculum does not promote sex. There is ample research to show that teaching students about their sexual health does not promote sex.

This is not a dumbed-down curriculum in which students learn about the efficacy of various contraceptives, not that such information is not also important; instead this curriculum is integrative in hopes of sending students back into the world outside the classroom with considered judgments, thoughts, and convictions. It is a democratic curriculum, based in liberal arts, that focuses on ethics and promotes caring. It focuses students on other people rather than themselves and in so doing, creates sexual citizens of character. I hope all readers will use and respond to the lessons online and help to take forward and expand this message about what sex ed can be, now and in the future, in caring schools.

CHAPTER 1

The Road to the Abstinence Debates

The subject is like nitroglycerine in that it must be handled with extreme caution or there will be an explosion which will wreck all the good intentions of the most progressive.

—Lowry, 1914, p. 26

What is missing from sex ed today? As you may have guessed from the introduction, lots. This has been the case in the United States for some time, and depending on the decade you are looking at, there are different kinds of absences. Today, however, there are specific, important absences that interfere with children's and adolescents' right to adequate information to make healthy decisions and their ability to become knowledgeable, responsible citizens in our democracy. The dumbing down of sex ed in the schools coupled with massive efforts to restrict the content delivered to students has resulted in the limited version of sex ed prevalent today. Even so-called Comprehensive Sex Ed (CSE) has been made less comprehensive as curricula are revised to meet current federal, state, and local requirements.

Still, a fair amount of sex ed takes place outside of the classroom. In the United States, we ironically live in a time when most adolescents will receive much more "comprehensive" sex education from multiple sources outside of school—the Internet, TV, movies, novels, friends, song lyrics, and so on. Some of that information is surprisingly accurate and informative. Point a teen to the right website and he or she can learn anything from pros and cons of different forms of contraception to a number of "how-tos" regarding typical and even atypical sex practices. We might ask then, "What responsibility do schools have in relation to this information and educating youths about sexuality?" And we might add to that question, given the amount of information available and given the hassles involved with implementing a sex ed program, why should schools even bother?

One answer to the first question has been that the schools should be responsible for providing basic health care information to students and that sex ed falls under the category of a kind of health care. This is because students who are not "healthy" in their sexual practices may end up with serious health or health-related issues, for example, STIs and pregnancy.

But another answer to both the first and second questions is that schools raise citizens. One main purpose of the public school system is to nurture good citizens in our society. To this end, sex ed should address not only the personal and health issues of adolescents, but the ways in which they can become and behave like good sexual citizens.

This book aims to present a new focus for sex education in the United States and thus it is not written only for sex educators, a group whose members have been trained for the most part to fit lessons into health class formats and emphasize either contraception or abstinence depending on the regulations for the state or district they teach in. It is also written for all stakeholders in adolescent sex ed: pre-service teachers, teachers, principals, board members, and parents. By clarifying who and what are at stake when we minimize sex ed and reduce it to a few health lessons, and coming to understand what broadening sex ed can achieve for our adolescents and society, stakeholders can make better arguments for truly comprehensive sex ed.

This book presents the perspective that a truly comprehensive sex education must address topics that extend beyond the individual and the personal. There are rampant problems in society that education can partly address. Sexual violence, unmonitored use of pornography at increasingly younger ages, the sexualization of childhood, and homophobic bullying are just a few of the problems that sex ed can and should address. While it is incredibly important for students to have access to health information with regard to contraception and facts and myths about a myriad of health-related issues, it is also crucial for them to have the time and space to discuss the version of sex and sexuality they see all around them and to discuss the ethics of sexual behavior.

A BRIEF HISTORY OF SEX ED, 1920s TO PRESENT

The brief history below describes the argument between Abstinence Only Until Marriage (AOUM) and Comprehensive Sex Education (CSE) advocates. A longer history would reveal how, for more than 100 years, ethics and values have played a significant role in much of the discourse surrounding sex ed. The Social Purity movement with its racist ideology spoke of values (Sethna, 2010), as did the Social Hygiene movement, which used "scientific facts" to promote healthy and sexually well-adjusted, marriageable youths (Luker, 2006; Moran, 2000). In the 1920s through the 1940s sex education attempted to produce youths who would be good marriage partners—marriage courses abounded (Moran, 2000). And in the 1950s into the 1960s, Family Life Sex Education (FLSE) courses assumed the position that sex education should be ethical education. It is important to note that the first "Family Relations" class was taught by a high school English teacher and purported to train girls and boys to be responsible parents and good marriage partners. FLSE courses were indeed comprehensive sex education courses, with a moral purpose; however, after the Kinsey reports of the 1950s and concomitant social changes in the United States, sex and marriage parted ways (Luker, 2006). Sex education changed to both address a so-called epidemic of teen pregnancy even though in the 1960s and 1970s there wasn't one (Greslé-Favier, 2010, p. 414), but this kind of curriculum and others were written in an attempt to "keep the lid on a sexual revolution that already was well underway" (Irvine, 2002, p. 20).

After 1965, FLSE programs became increasingly popular across the country and were present in the curriculum from K–12. This indeed was a heyday of comprehensive sex education that included not only the mechanics of reproduction but also ethics in co-ed classrooms. These programs also promoted a teaching style associated with the 1960s that purported to engage students in their own thinking, a "student-centered" approach that involved discussion and debate while teachers would take a morally neutral stance. In these classrooms students held moral debates and evaluated behaviors in terms of moral goals such as preventing "exploitation of others" (Moran, 2000, p. 175). In the most famous of these curricula, the Anaheim FLSE curriculum, there were lessons on homosexuality, masturbation, contraception, and intercourse. It even spoke of the pleasure of sexual intercourse.

But three years after the Anaheim curriculum began to be taught in the public schools, a woman, Eleanor Howe, formed a local group of Mothers Organized for Moral Stability and protested the curriculum for its lack of moral language, discussions of homosexuality and masturbation, and the explicit illustrations. This protest was taken up nationally by fundamentalist Christian and educator Gordon Drake, who had ties to the John Birch Society—the John Birch Society is an extreme right-wing society founded in 1958 that has become known today for its opposition to the civil rights movement and anti-Semitism (John Birch Society, 2010). Birch's pamphlet, "Is the Schoolhouse the Proper Place to Teach Raw Sex?," sold 90,000 copies. It contained complaints about the immoral nature of sex education and lies regarding the results of the Anaheim course—that it caused "venereal disease," the word used for STIs in those times, and that it caused pregnancy rates to rise (when VD and pregnancy were actually declining). This movement also produced inflammatory news stories about how these classes sent girls and boys into closets to "explore" one another and even how one sex ed teacher was raped by overstimulated male students (Moran, 2000, p. 181).

By 1969, during the first term of President Richard M. Nixon, there were arguments over sex education in over 30 states (Moran, 2000, p. 184). These arguments continued on and took hold in the 1980s through the dissemination of Abstinence Only and Abstinence Only Until Marriage curricula.

"Values education" got a bad reputation as a method in which students were permitted to freely choose whatever sexual values they wanted to have. And relativism in values became associated with FLSE curricula rather than the idea that students need and deserve a place for intelligent and ethical discussion about the sexuality they see around them and the sexual issues that are a part of their lives and the lives of those in their growing interpersonal spheres.

By 2008, our government had spent over $1.5 billion on abstinence education (Advocates for Youth, 2007). This money, instead of being directed toward social problems directly impacting the health of adolescents, went instead to programs that did little to deliver the very information intrinsically tied to health outcomes. What a critical pedagogy perspective shows is that sex ed is as much influenced by the politics of the times as it is by real concern for adolescents.

How did we get to this content-poor and ethically questionable state of affairs in sex ed? The 1980s and 1990s saw a growth of legislation and federal influence on sex education. When President Ronald Reagan first funded abstinence-only education he did so only minimally and left the main decisions about sex ed to states and community groups, not wanting big government to get involved (Kendall, 2008b). That 1981 legislation, the Adolescent Family Life (AFL) Title XX bill, seemed not to be a problem for progressive sex educators given that in the late 1980s only 1 in 50 sex education programs taught abstinence only (Dailard, 2001). By the late 1990s, however, 86% of schools required that abstinence be promoted as either the only or preferred means of contraception (Kendall, 2008b; Landry, Kaeser, & Richards, 1999). And, since 1996, the federal government has provided more than $1.5 billion for AOUM programming (Advocates for Youth, 2007; Kendall, 2008b). AOUM programming was even required in international initiatives (Kendall, 2008b). By 1999, one in four teachers taught AOUM and six states required condemning abortion and homosexuality in their curricula (Kendall, 2008b, p. 24).

The Move toward AOUM

The change from minimal support for abstinence curricula to the beginning of a new era in which abstinence-only curricula became a requirement for federal funding began during a Democrat's administration, under Bill Clinton, when, in Section 510 of the Personal Responsibility and Work Opportunity Reconciliation Act of 1996, the president signed a bill that gave $50 million a year in federal grants to states for AOUM education (Dailard, 2005). States had to match every $4 of funding they received from the national government with $3 of their own in order to access this money, but over time, when states found that these programs were not effective, many began to refuse this funding and search for alternative funding sources (LeCroy & Milligan Associates, 2003).

The initial funding to the states enacted in 1996 laid out an eight-point definition of abstinence (the eight tenets referred to below) and instructed that a program could emphasize any of them as long as it also didn't contradict any (Santelli et al., 2006). The eight tenets said that each federally funded AOUM program should:

1. Have as its exclusive purpose teaching the social, psychological, and health gains to be realized by abstaining from sexual activity;
2. Teach abstinence from sexual activity outside marriage as the expected standard for all school-age children;
3. Teach that abstinence from sexual activity is the only certain way to avoid out-of-wedlock pregnancy, sexually transmitted diseases, and other associated health problems;
4. Teach that a mutually faithful, monogamous relationship in the context of marriage is the expected standard of sexual activity;
5. Teach that sexual activity outside the context of marriage is likely to have harmful psychological and physical effects;
6. Teach that bearing children out of wedlock is likely to have harmful consequences for the child, the child's parents, and society;
7. Teach young people how to reject sexual advances and how alcohol and drug use increases vulnerability to sexual advances;
8. Teach the importance of attaining self-sufficiency before engaging in sexual activity (Section 510[b] of Title V, Section 510 (b)(2)(A-H) of the Social Security Act, P.L. 104–193).

The national growth of these programs was supported by another bill, passed in 2001, known as the Children and Families Community-Based Abstinence-Education (CBAE) Program. This legislation made available even more funding for AOUM programming, funding that bypassed states and gave directly to organizations that were, for example, faith-based or that provided pregnancy crisis services. Money was provided to community organizations as long as they provided AOUM education to 12- to 18-year-olds and as long as they followed the eight tenets of AOUM education laid out in the 1996 bill. While the initially legislated funding remained at $50 million a year after 1996, CBAE funding increased this to $115 million in 2006. From 2006 until the Obama administration, all the growth in funding was accounted for by the CBAE program (Fine & McClelland, 2006; Santelli et al., 2006).

With the new eight tenets, programs were not permitted to provide information about contraception. Moreover, in 2006, the objectives that earlier were described as discouraging "premature sexual activity" and to support "abstinence decisions" were changed to read more conservatively to discourage "*premarital* sexual activity" and encourage "*abstinence-until-marriage* decisions" (Dailard, 2005).

The Satcher Report

This growth in AOUM funding occurred in spite of Surgeon General David Satcher's report, released in 2001, about 7 months before his term expired in February 2002. The report reviewed the scientific literature on sex education and ended with a call for comprehensive sex education (Satcher, 2001). Satcher argued that scientific evidence showed that CSE is effective and that efficacy is what parents wanted for their teens. In his report he listed the goals of sex education as including "the ability to understand and weigh the risks, responsibilities, outcomes and impacts of sexual actions and to practice abstinence when appropriate," and "freedom from sexual abuse and discrimination and the ability of individuals to integrate their sexuality into their lives, derive pleasure from it, and to reproduce if they so choose" (Satcher, 2001, p. 1). An interesting thread that ran through this report concerned sexual violence as a public health issue, which is not always part of the discourse today with regard to sex education and one that I would like to see returned to curricula. The report said that 22 percent of all women have been victims of forced sexual acts and that 104,000 children are victims of sexual abuse each year. The report also indicated, importantly, that sexuality could not be altered through force of will.

Satcher's report was met with criticism from conservative forces such as Peter Brandt, the director of Focus on the Family, a church-based conservative group, which called the report "ideology disguised as science from the beginning to the end" (Schemo, 2001). Nevertheless, it remains, for advocates of CSE, a bright point in the history of sex education in the 21st century.

The phrase "comprehensive sexuality" began to be used more widely in the early 1990s as an alternative form of sex education to AOUM. SIECUS first put out its *Guidelines for Comprehensive Sexuality Education* in 1991 and began to use the term "sexuality education" rather than "sex education" to send the message that comprehensive education included many aspects of what it means to be a sexual person and not just teachings about how and when and with whom to have sex. Satcher's report, thus, was perceived as very sympathetic toward a CSE agenda. Nevertheless, it would take more than a surgeon general's report to stop the growth of the AOUM agenda.

Evidence-Based Arguments

In the late 20th and early 21st century, a movement for evidence-based strategies gained momentum in the social sciences, in the field of education, in the treatment of psychological disorders, and in government policy. This phrase "evidence-based" was used to signify that considerable research had suggested that the strategy was effective and even preferred to other strategies. Those opponents of AOUM education used this strategy to combat its widespread use. Douglas Kirby (2001, 2007) produced an analysis of the effectiveness of a majority of the programs in preventing pregnancy and/or STIs.

After Kirby's first analysis (2001), liberal legislators in Congress produced a report that documented the inaccuracies in abstinence curricula. Called the Waxman Report (2004), this study found that two-thirds of government funded AOUM programs contained misleading or inaccurate information. Also, a very powerful report published by Mathematica Policy Research (Trenholm, Devaney, Fortson, Quay, Wheeler & Clark, 2007) that took 9 years to complete showed longitudinal data following middle and elementary school children through four different extensive abstinence programs until they were about 16 years of age, comparing these students to a control group. These data indicated that their age of first intercourse was no different than those teens who did not have AOUM programming and that they had a similar number of partners, got STIs at the same rate, used condoms at the same rate, and basically had the same amount of knowledge regarding the effectiveness of condoms. A report on sex ed in the state of Texas with regard to its sex education followed suit, claiming that little material beyond abstinence was taught and the materials used contained numerous factual errors (Wiley & Wilson, 2009). The Kirby study of 2007, *Emerging Answers*, along with these other studies, fueled organizations such as SIECUS, Advocates for Youth, the ACLU, and Planned Parenthood Federation in their campaign for comprehensive sex education.

The AOUM supporters responded with a small review of nine CSE curricula. This review, produced by the Administration for Children and Families and the Department of Health and Human Services (2007), showed that the curricula were more effective in increasing condom use than delaying first sex and that the percentage of accurate material in these curricula was similar to the percentage of accuracy of AOUM curricula.

Still, the damage had been done and by 2007 AOUM programs were on the chopping block largely due to these evidence-based attacks. State health departments began rejecting abstinence education and state legislatures in Colorado, Iowa, and Washington passed laws that made it difficult to keep teaching these curricula (Beil, 2007). In 2007, AOUM programs experienced their first cut in Senate financing since 2001 (Beil, 2007). In 2009, half the states declined Title V AOUM funding (Boonstra, 2010).

Interestingly, research at the time showed that teenagers were abstaining more and that those who weren't abstaining were more likely to use contraception. These trends might suggest that the AOUM programs were working and successful in their purpose, but data show that the trend began years before AOUM programming became popular. Ever since 1991, pregnancy and birth rates have been falling. Also of interest is that the state in which AOUM education has been incredibly popular and which received the most funding, Texas, had the smallest decline in pregnancy; but Texas received almost $17 million for abstinence education (Beil, 2007).

Sex Ed Today

Studies have examined AOUM curricula's effectiveness or lack thereof, compared their effectiveness to the effectiveness of CSE curricula, Evidence-Based (EB) curricula, or Abstinence-Plus (abstinence *and* comprehensive information about sex) curricula. Moreover, a congressional report, the Waxman Report (2004), was released, documenting the misinformation in these curricula. In spite of this science, advocates of a comprehensive sex education have been working around constraints and agendas sometimes quite foreign to their purpose and scientific understanding in order to get the funding and permission needed to provide teens and pre-teens with reliable information about their own sexual development. They have rarely been given the breathing room, let alone the grant money, to imagine what sex education *could* be like beyond social skills training that would lead to scientifically measurable outcomes such as the delay of first sex and the reduction of teen pregnancy and STIs.

When President Obama took office he promised to "restore science to its rightful place" (Obama, 2009), referring to a number of problems including AOUM education. It wasn't until 2011, however, that Democratic congressional leaders Lautenberg and Lee introduced the Repealing Ineffective and Incomplete Abstinence-Only Program Funding Act. This legislation redirects funding from AOUM programs to pregnancy prevention programs and the Personal Responsibility Education Program (PREP), which funds CSE and EB programs at the state level. All funded programs need to be evidence based, medically accurate, and age appropriate, but not all need to be comprehensive. The pregnancy prevention programs need to teach about abstinence *and* contraception, and the PREP programs are to add subjects like financial literacy, parent-child communication, and decision making. In this way, family life may be re-entering curricula. The PREP program gives over $5 million each year to states for programs that aim to prevent pregnancy and STIs, and doesn't require matching funds from the state (Boonstra, 2010). The Teen Pregnancy Prevention Program gives over $114 million to states. It is important to remember, however, that Congress also elected in 2010 to keep AOUM funding for another 5 years, so $50 million is still available to states that want to continue to use AOUM curricula.

A RETURN TO FAMILY VALUES?

The phrase "family values" may be forever lost to liberals after social conservatives began to use it to describe Christian values. In this book, however, I argue that teaching ethics (and I use the term "ethics" to point to something more universal and supported than "values," which seem to me to be closer to family preferences) is fundamental to democratic education. A truly democratic education produces a democratic citizen. That is, democratic ethical education should not only point students inward, to develop moral arguments for their beliefs and opinions, but outward to develop moral practices toward the people with whom they will have sex, talk about sex, and influence sexually. It should also point students even further outward to the world around them and help them to develop positions and moral thinking about sexual events and issues in modern society.

The kind of training and classrooms necessary for this kind of education is suggested by the field of moral education. By emphasizing moral reasoning as well as empathy, we create responsible thinkers and moral actors. To produce thoughtful, moral citizens, in an increasingly sexualized world in which myriad sexual content is readily accessible to adolescents, sex education needs to engage students in reasonable debate about sexual issues, themes, and dilemmas that are a part of modern society and not just their own high school worlds.

My hope is that pre-service teachers will heed this call and not only advocate for a more humanities- and social science–based curriculum in their middle schools and high schools but integrate this kind of ethical perspective on sex and sexual development as it arises in the traditional content courses they teach.

I want to acknowledge that authors of AOUM curricula, because they do not focus on health, have had the opportunity to develop curricula that assume a fuller perspective of the student in context. AOUM authors attempt to speak to the whole child as a developing human being in a changing world. I don't agree with their view of what constitutes the whole child, a view that stereotypes gender and sees the child as battling shameful urges, but I do acknowledge the value of their broad focus.

There have been major causes to work for, but progressives have let teens down (or, have been forced by politics to let teens down?) by presenting very narrow, skills-focused, health-oriented curricula. While AOUM curricula have managed to incorporate discussions of pleasure, media, and gender relations, albeit confined within a very small world and Christian view, CSE and EB curricula authors (whose work is used in schools) have limited themselves to relaying health-related facts, as if these facts are valueless and the rest of what a teen does, thinks, and desires doesn't matter.

Adolescents, Erik Erikson has shown us, are loyal, imaginative risk takers (in acts and thinking), ready to devote themselves to strong causes, with full access to an emotional life that fuels them. Rather than the randy, hormonal, confused troublemakers or innocents whose impulsivity prevents them from making good decisions, I choose to see teens not as people to control, but as people to inspire and be inspired by. They certainly can and do inspire me with their energy and devotion. They are people with friendships, talents, and interests in the world around them. If we think of them as moral human beings ready to argue, fight, and invest, we can see them as citizens already. As Dewey argued, the enterprise of education is development, the creation of citizens. Sex education can conceptualize teens as future citizens, as people ready to understand what's at stake in their treatment of others with whom they have sex, and what's at stake in their attitudes and understandings regarding sex and sexual relationships, from not only a personal perspective but a social and a moral perspective.

CHAPTER 2

A Critical View of Trends
in Sex Ed: 12 Issues

The history of sex education unfolds as a series of critiques and revisions, some coming from conservatives, some from liberals, and some from folks in the middle. Because AOUM was the mode of programming supported during the 1990s and 2000s, subsequent critiques focus on the inadequacy of that education. However, some of the same critiques leveled at AOUM curricula could be easily leveled at a number of other kinds of curricula as well. This chapter reviews the problems with "sex ed today"—actually, not just today but also during the 1990s and 2000s. AOUM education is not alone in its inadequacy; the current narrow liberal conceptualization of what sex education can and should be is also problematic. Curricula typically don't mirror ideals but instead reflect compromises. Still, they are the texts and messages with which young people will invariably grapple, and criticism of their messages constitutes one method critical pedagogy employs to reveal the biases and power hierarchies that ultimately influence the education of youth. How, then, do critics do their work? For the most part, critics read and analyze what they read. If you were given a sex education curriculum and asked to critique it you might not know where to start. Critics begin with an idea about what is problematic in current popular ideas about sex. They also begin with the problems they see in the curricula they review. For example, a critic might wonder whether curricula reflect the heterosexism that seems so prevalent in public discourse about sexuality. Or a critic might be interested in gender stereotypes and want to review a curriculum to examine if it contains any. My students and I did just that and the results are below in the section on stereotypes. One of the hunches that motivated me to write a sexual ethics curriculum was that sex education was becoming too focused on the individual and not the relationship, so my analysis examines when and where curricula talk about the other person or a partner.

Nancy Lesko has an interesting take on the kind of criticism I'm talking about. She describes this kind of criticism as a criticism of "discovery," a criticism that promises to unveil the "structured, hegemonic, 'really true' nature of knowledge production, circulation, and consumption" (Lesko, 2010, p. 282). She criticizes this approach and suggests that we examine materials while considering the affects they evoke in us or students. "Exposure" or "discovery" analysis, she claims, leads the discoverer or reader toward satisfaction, a sense of superiority, or even a sense of outrage. Reading material for affect can, however, summon a host of emotions, and Lesko reads curricula to explore what she names as "nostalgic longings" and whether or not the curricula "touch," or move us emotionally, in any way.

Thus, it seems important to pay attention not only to the exposure criticisms below, but also, in Chapter 3, to examine the kinds of moral feelings and moral directions the curricula intend for us to feel and follow.

The following are summaries of 12 criticisms of sex ed today. The final criticism regards the lack of moral focus and the concentration on the individual and leads to suggestions for future curricula in Chapters 5 and 6.

AOUM CURRICULA DO NOT ACKNOWLEDGE THAT TEENS ARE HAVING SEX

The lack of acknowledgement in some curricula that teens are, in fact, having sex makes the information these curricula provide inadequate. Ethically this leaves young people at risk. It also doesn't support a basic right of autonomy with regard to health consequences; that is, we are withholding information from them that would make a difference in the health decisions they make.

In 2000, the Kaiser Family Foundation as well as Douglas Kirby (2001), a major researcher of sex education curricula, separately made claims that the programs that were being used in schools were often irrelevant to adolescents. They were primarily criticizing AOUM sex ed programs that, adhering to the eight tenets of AOUM education, left out of their curricula any information about how to use birth control and how to protect oneself from STIs by means other than abstinence. By doing so, they and others like them argued that these curricula leave students who are having sex with no knowledge or tools for decision making. For example, Trudell and Whatley (1991) reviewed *Sex Respect* and argued that the authors seemed out of touch with the reality that over half of teens have had sexual intercourse by the age of 17. Whatley and Trudell (1993) turned their eyes toward a second curriculum, *Teen Aid,* and found that material on contraception was almost entirely lacking, while material on abortion, much of it biased against abortion, was plentiful. Collins, Alagiri, Summers, and Morin (2002) wrote that "Abstinence-only programming runs the serious risk of leaving young people, especially those at elevated risk, uninformed and alienated" (p. 8). Some critics have even raised the question of whether or not it is unethical to withhold health information from adolescents, health information that may make a big difference in their lives (Santelli et al., 2006). They take a "human rights" approach to sexual health information and argue that governments have "an obligation to provide accurate information to their citizens and eschew the provision of misinformation" (p. 85).

The fact was and is that many adolescents do have intercourse and engage in other forms of potentially dangerous sexual contact, although "dangerous" is not the only way to describe these activities (CDC, 2011; Kaiser Family Foundation, 2011). While national rates of teen sexual activity have declined over the past decade, still about half of all high school teens will report having had sex by the end of their senior year, and more than one in five report having had four or more partners by the time they graduate from high school. One-quarter of sexually active adolescents nationwide have an STI, many of which are viral infections with no cure.

Still, those who insist in their criticism of adolescents' right to information have concerns beyond the prevention of harm. Liberals have reached a general consensus that knowledge supports freedom, subjectivity, agency, and responsibility, and the withholding of knowledge works against such agency (Santelli et al., 2006; Tolman, 2000, 2002). With regard to subjectivity, theorists write that to be a subject rather than an object means to have a voice, to care about what happens to oneself, and to be able to make decisions on behalf of one's own health without being overpowered by another's needs or by what peers think and do (Tolman, 2002). As Fine wrote, anti-sex rhetoric "does little to enhance the development of sexual responsibility and subjectivity in adolescents" (1988, p. 29).

Withholding information about contraception also doesn't concur with what most parents of teens want. Parents and other adults do seem to realize that teens are going to have sex. A Kaiser Family Foundation survey showed that the majority of parents wanted their adolescent students to have a comprehensive sex education (2000). The National Campaign to Prevent Teen Pregnancy released a study in 2001 that showed that while 95% of adults thought receiving a strong abstinence message was important for teens, 70% of them said that advising abstinence while also giving young people information about contraception is not a mixed message (Kirby, 2001)

The answer for all parties concerned about adolescents who *do* or *might* have sex is comprehensive sex education, one that includes both abstinence as well as accurate information about STIs, contraception, and sexual practices. This indeed was what former Surgeon General David Satcher recommended before he left office (Satcher, 2001). However, AOUM education advocates continue to promote the belief that any message about what adolescents should do when they eventually have sex is a message that suggests that they ought to be having sex.

TEEN SEX IS STEREOTYPED
AND DESCRIBED ONLY AS A PROBLEM

Over a hundred years ago, Hall described adolescence as a time of *sturm und drang*—storm and stress (1904). This view was reintroduced in the 1960s to describe adolescence as rocky and a reason for the so-called "generation gap." This view is also more currently supported by a medical-physiological perspective regarding hormones, which supposedly produce erratic and emotional behavior. A third and typical way of viewing adolescent turbulence derives from psychoanalytic theory, which describes adolescence as a time of negotiating separation from parents. As Bay-Cheng, referencing Lesko, notes, "the discursive intersection between adolescence and sexuality yields a fundamental assumption: teens are hypersexual, their lives driven by sexual desire and impulses" (Bay-Cheng, 2003, p. 62). She argues that this assumption reduces sex "to a decontextualized, disembodied state."

Many have noted that this view of adolescents as hypersexual and needing to be tamed positions them as people to be controlled and monitored. Schools in particular treat adolescent sex as a problem to be managed (Allen 2005; Rasmussen, 2004). Ashcraft (2006) agrees that teens are assumed to be immature, irresponsible, and in denial regarding the consequences of sex.

Biology also rears its head in discussions of "timing" that center around the right time to "do it." Critic Janssen (2009) writes, "In the 1990s U.S. we have witnessed a veritable cult of the age-appropriate, a Quest for the Normal" (p. 6). He points out that "first sex" or "debut sex" is "a highly pivotal parameter in health research and is crucial to American notions of abstinence and virginity pledging" (p. 7). As Janssen (2009) puts it, "virginity seems to be a durable site for pedagogical intervention" (p. 16). This focus on first sex as intercourse implies that all other sex, from playing with oneself as a small child to the mutual masturbation of adolescents, is not sex at all. Janssen (2009) calls this the "cult of the first experience" (p. 7). Ashcraft (2006) examines this phenomenon also, calling it a discourse of readiness. Curricula as well as websites, teen magazines, and popular TV shows, like *Glee*, focus on whether or not one is "ready" for the big step of heterosexual vaginal intercourse. Such heterosexist portrayals of sexuality are also problematic in that they direct sex education toward a sole aspect of a student's sexual development, expression, or choices.

TEENS ARE REPRESENTED AS CHILDREN IN DANGER OF BEING LURED INTO HARMFUL EXPERIENCES

The practice of policing adolescents stems from the belief that if teens are exposed to the evils of world, they will be ruined (Janssen, 2009, p. 18). It's easy to laugh at things in the past that parents thought were influencing their children in negative ways—pool halls; the jitterbug; the Beatles—but to be fair to parents of yesteryear, it is also important to realize that at the time, parents weren't thinking those teen interests were bad in and of themselves, but bad because of the attitudes they induced.

Today, parents and some sex ed curricula authors want to save adolescents from the media's influence, including lyrics that are sexist and sexual as well as parts of pop culture that treat sex as casual and represent it in ways that evoke mainstream pornography. In general, the means by which we protect students from the potential bad influence of such things is to keep those materials out of their hands. The problem with this approach, common sense tells us, is that any warning that something is "not for kids" draws kids to the material. The recording industry, along with the porn industry, spends billions of dollars trying to lure teens in to buy their products, and make their products a part of their lifestyle so that teens will be consumers for life (Dines, 2010; Levin & Kilbourne, 2008). Because parents can't turn off the world, teens will need to develop critical thinking and a moral perspective of what they are viewing and consuming.

CURRICULA STILL CONTAIN INACCURACIES

The Waxman Report was commissioned by Democrats in the legislature to review AOUM curricula, and the report found that of the 13 curricula reviewed, 80% of the curricular material contained "false, misleading, or distorted information about reproductive health" (Waxman, 2004). The most common inaccuracies reported were the gross underestimation of the effectiveness of condoms in preventing pregnancy and STIs, false claims about physical and psychological risks of abortion, inaccuracies about the incidence and transmission of STIs, religious belief and gender role stereotypes presented as scientific fact, and in general a number of scientific errors (Waxman, 2004).

Wilson et al. (2005) found considerable variability in AOUM programs, although the curricular content generally reflected "ideological beliefs, political climate, and market moods" (p. 97). In Wilson et al.'s study, none of the 21 curricula reviewed received an "excellent" on ratings of accuracy, and the inaccuracies manifested themselves in the form of amusing quotes such as the following: "the outward direction of sperm cells is supported by emphasis on an outward direction in the male personality. . . . The ovum, by contrast, is receptive and inward-directed . . . the female personality is generally more receptive and inward than the male's" (Wilson et al., 2005, p. 96). This quote reflects earlier work by Whatley and Trudell (1993), who discuss how the curriculum authors mix scientific concepts and definitions with biased information, giving false statistics (e.g., how condoms break in 50% of cases involving male homosexual activity).

HETEROSEXIST BIAS PERMEATES MANY CURRICULA

Abstinence Only Until Marriage curricula along with the Abstinence-Plus curricula that arose in competition with the AOUM curricula to give students contraception information *in case they did not make the preferred choice of abstinence* focused on vaginal, sexual intercourse as sex. Bay-Cheng (2003) writes that in these curricula, "normality is located within a *monogamous, coitus-centered* relationship between a man and a woman both of whom generally conform to *conventional gender roles*" (p. 67). Bay-Cheng also claims that these curricula treat queer sexuality not merely as LGBTQ identity, but as a pathologized sexuality.

Trudell and Whatley (1991) found that those AOUM curricula, like *Sex Respect,* that included discussion of HIV/AIDS characterized the disease as a punishment, consistent with some fundamentalist Christian views of the time. They note that the 1986 version of the curriculum described AIDS and herpes as nature's way of "making some kind of a comment on sexual behavior" (p. 4).

Normative sexual behavior is quite frequently described in school-based sex education curricula as vaginal intercourse between a man and a woman (Elia, 2000; Kiely, 2005; Redman, 1994). This assumption of a heterosexual relationship in sex ed curricula has been a problem in sex education for a very long time (Holland, Ramazanoglu, Sharpe, & Thomson, 1998). Research with boys and girls in high schools suggests that they also tend to assume the view that intercourse is the "real" form of sex, even after alternative perspectives are presented (Jackson & Weatherall, 2010). Wilson et al. (2005) point out that this narrow conceptualization of sex is not unique to AOUM curricula but occurs in comprehensive curricula as well. However, AOUM curricula marginalize same-sex relationships even further than comprehensive curricula by declaring that sex is only healthy or appropriate within a marital relationship. There is rarely mention of same-sex relationships in these discussions, much less an explanation of how to have an "approved" sexual relationship when marriage is not granted to same-sex couples in most states.

When sex is portrayed only as intercourse, LGBTQ students' needs and concerns are invisible in the classroom (Lensky, 1990). Rasmussen (2004) argues that educating for pleasure provides a counter-narrative to LGBTQ students with regard to what she calls "wounded identities," and encourages students and teachers to think beyond heteronormative categories. She also argues that what gives pleasure should not define identity (Rasmussen, 2004). Queering sex education would make it anti-heteronormative and non-homophobic. Lesbian, gay, bisexual, transgender, or queer sexualities rarely appear in school-based curricula (Buston & Hart, 2001; Redman, 1994), and when they are represented, they tend to be marginalized (Whatley, 1999).

One solution to heterosexist bias is to not assign gender or name to characters in vignettes or scenarios stated. *Reducing the Risk* introduces characters with gender-neutral names like Lee, Chris, and Pat as examples, thereby allowing students to envision conversations about sex as occurring between heterosexual and same-sex couples. Moreover, the gender neutrality means that males are not always represented as the sexually assertive party in interactions. Using these names advances the ethic that the information for sex is given to all students, no matter their orientation, and that the problems that arise for adolescents apply universally. This strategy works for the most part in many of the conversations/role plays, but when Lee gets pregnant and has a baby, which prevents her from attending the sophomore dance, it is fairly clear that she is female, and her partner is male.

Other curricula like the *Our Whole Lives* (*OWL*) and *Family Life and Sexual Health* (*FLASH*) curricula, which are not school-based, are unusual in that they teach directly about inclusivity (Goldfarb & Casparian, 2000; Reis et al., 2011). These kinds of curricula contain units on sexual orientation that address discrimination and bullying and explain stereotypes. Both of these curricula discuss why and where people "come out" and how a heterosexual student might become an ally. The rationale for these units contains moral language of responsibility and obligation: Schools have an *obligation* to enhance every student's self-esteem and to enhance

relationships in all kinds of families; they are obligated to counteract stereotyping and discrimination; and they are obligated to provide a safe
environment for learning to all students. Rather than avoid the most
controversial discussions, these authors have optional homework assignments where students are asked to explore their values by talking with an
adult they trust with regard to same-sex sex, and topics such as same-sex
parenting, adoption, job discrimination, and attempts to change sexual
orientation through therapy. The *OWL* curriculum, by integrating both
religion and social justice issues, and by asking students to become allies,
provides a sex education perspective that covers issues that extend beyond
personal decision making with regard to whether or not to have sex. The
FLASH and *OWL* curricula stand apart from other curricula in that they
address value-laden social issues, one component of which is sex.

Several other curricula speak directly about the inclusion of LGBTQ
youth, although AOUM curricula are notorious for exclusion (Fisher,
2009) and misinformation (Henneman, 2005). The AOUM curriculum,
Sex Respect, received substantial criticism for its treatment of "homosexual activity" in its lesson on HIV/AIDS. In earlier editions, the authors
wrote that "In such activity, body openings are used in ways for which
they are not designed. During such unnatural behaviors, additional damage is done to blood vessels and other body parts" (Mast, 1986, p. 52).
This demeaning and inaccurate language contributes to the creation of
an unsafe environment for non-heterosexual youths and makes them
ashamed if not angry and upset.

Abstinence Clearinghouse claims to provide medically accurate
educational materials and training for abstinence-only education programs. SIECUS (2008), in their Community Action Kit, examines the
Abstinence Clearinghouse message that states that, while "emotional
intimacy" is an "innate need" for everyone, "sexual activity does not
replace true intimacy" and "friendship with another person of the same
sex" does not require physical intimacy to "validate" it. The statement
continues, "research shows the homosexual lifestyle is not a healthy
alternative for males or females" in that our bodies are not "anatomi-
cally suited" for homosexual acts, which are "very dangerous for disease" (SIECUS, 2008). Abstinence Clearinghouse has since removed this
information from their website, www.abstinence.net.

Most AOUM sex ed "erases the existence of GLBTQ youth," according
to Henneman (2005, p. 58) and supported by Fisher (2009). Pro-absti-
nence organizations are successful at censoring lessons in sex education
curricula deemed to be gay-friendly (Henneman, 2005). Martha Kempner,
head of SIECUS, reminds us how even if some of the more "overt [anti-
gay] biases" have been addressed, "subtle" messages remain, for example,

teaching to wait until marriage to have sex—in a state that does not allow gay marriage—shows certain bias (Henneman, 2005, p. 58). Such an approach "reifies heteronormativity through an active silence" (Fisher, 2009, p. 75).

The reasons behind critics' arguments for inclusion extend beyond politics and the desire for democracy. Exclusion becomes a health issue when teens who do not engage in heteronormative sexual practice are not told about safety practices that might affect them. A curriculum that moves beyond heteronormativity must do more than simply acknowledge various sexual identities; it must also discuss other kinds of sex as pleasurable, sometimes even more pleasurable than coitus, and as safe, sometimes safer than alternatives.

A WHITE, MIDDLE-CLASS BIAS STILL EXISTS

Racial discrimination is the focus of one important critique of sex education today (Fields, 2005, 2008). Jessica Fields' ethnography of a North Carolina school system's disputes over sex education examines the discourse of advocates of AOUM curricula, and finds a subtle (and sometimes not so subtle) view that African American girls' sexuality is corrupt. Fields found in her research that AOUM advocates would state unfounded research that 20% of kids were "unsalvageable" with regard to whether or not they would go on to have sex in their teens, and used coded talk about "children having children" to mask talk about African American and low-income girls without actually mentioning race or class.

African American women's sexuality has frequently and historically been represented as excessive and deviant (Collins, 2000; Rose, 2005), and Fields demonstrates how the talk between the AOUM advocates reflects this history. Fields also discusses the liberal response to the conservative discourse around African American girlhood that strives to show compassion for them as girls and not adultify them as problematic over-sexualized adults who will soon be in the welfare system. This way of talking about the African American girls reminded others that these girls are "innocent," too, the way European American suburban girls have been depicted. But Fields "troubles" this idea of childhood sexual innocence. She notes that liberals also retained racialized notions of African Americans by blaming mothers in poverty as poor role models, even while acknowledging that economic conditions prevent mothers from adequately supervising their daughters. They concluded that schools need to intervene where parents fail. In this way, the liberals in the town chose the path of "saving the little girls" rather than the avenue of providing family support, which might entail programs that directly involve parents or those that seek to address the sexuality of young men. Fields writes, "The rhetoric of African American girls as sexual innocents is a no-less-constraining possibility, despite its promise of moral standing, social protection, and concern" (Fields, 2005, p. 568).

Early on, Trudell and Whatley (1991) also explored racism by examining the illustrations in curricula and found that most of the pictures of youths were of White youths. This no longer seems to be the case. However, some critics debate whether the inclusive illustrations in AOUM curricula were a concerted attempt to target Black urban youths, and whether or not Black urban or White middle-class suburban areas were targeted for AOUM curricula (Kendall, 2008b).

PLEASURE IS ABSENT AND EMPOWERMENT NEGLECTED

This criticism has perhaps been the critique that has engendered the most writing about sex education. Issues of pleasure and the right to pleasure have sparked enormous interest among feminists, LGBTQ authors and researchers, and liberals in general. Since Michelle Fine's important 1988 piece, "The Missing Discourse of Desire," a tremendous amount of work has analyzed where and why this discourse is missing and also what happens when it is brought up. In general, critics note that pleasure is not recognized as a part of sex in sex education (Allen, 2007a, 2007b; Fine, 1988; Harrison, Hillier, & Walsh, 1996; Holland et al. 1998; Kiely, 2005; Rasmussen, 2004). When it appears, it seems to "perpetuate dominant discourses of male and female heterosexuality" (Allen, 2007b, p. 250). In addition, Diorio and Munro (2003) point out that illustrations of the female "reproductive" system often omit the clitoris as a site for female pleasure.

The absence of pleasure talk (and illustrations including the clitoris) is seen as particularly detrimental to young women because it reinforces societal standards of passivity for women during sex, and the idea that if and when women are permitted to be sexual, it is in the service of entertaining or pleasing men. Thus the inclusion of lessons on sexual pleasure could support female sexual entitlement to pleasure. Some argue that when a woman feels entitled to sexual pleasure, she is better able to make choices about sex and to say no to it (Allen, 2008; Tolman, 2002). Tolman and Higgins (1996) propose that pleasure is associated with being a "bad girl" and the idea of the "good girl" influences girls to be less assertive in resisting sexual coercion and, as a result, limits their ability to explain what happened to them in accounts of sexual coercion.

Very rarely is the specific concern of female pleasure and entitlement addressed. But in *Be Proud! Be Responsible!* (Jemmott, Jemmott, & McCaffree, 1996), a CSE and EB curriculum, the authors write that "Most women need to have their clitoris touched directly or indirectly in order to have an orgasm," (p. 128) that sexual intercourse is not the only way for couples to get together, and that "touching and stroking can be pleasurable" (p. 128). They add not to rush and to "get to know your and your partner's body" (p. 128). This unusual but specific talk seems directly related to possibilities of pleasure for adolescent girls. The authors do indicate that achieving orgasm through touching alone is safer than through intercourse and describe how having sex using a condom can still be pleasurable. In this way, however, they, too, couch talk of pleasure in directions about safety. It is rare to find a discussion of pleasure for pleasure's sake.

Our Whole Lives, (*OWL*), known to be a progressive curriculum primarily offered through the Unitarian Universalist Church, also includes a piece in which female pleasure seems important. "Once the condom is removed" they write, "the man may relax with and hold his partner, or continue to pleasure his partner without further penetration with the penis" (Goldfarb & Casparian, 2000, p. 87). The use of the phrase "his partner" rather than "the girl" or "the woman" makes this passage applicable to gay sex also. However, the idea of pleasuring someone after you yourself are done seems to have particular importance for female sexual satisfaction.

Allen (2007b) discusses whether pleasure is indeed "teachable" or whether it is instead a "natural" or "private" part of life. With regard to how private sex today is, she describes how students in Western countries are "saturated with depictions of pleasurable sexualities in popular cultural forms like music videos, media advertising and television programmes" (p. 250). Allen also comments that the dominance of lessons about dangers wipes out any talk about the pleasure sex can bring.

AOUM curricula often associate pleasure with danger, when pleasure is discussed at all. For example, in *Choosing the Best Journey* (Cook, 2006), pleasure is associated with peer pressure. One boy says to a girl, "It's fun—you'll enjoy it" (p. 55, student version), and another says to a girl who refuses, "we can take things slow I promise. But I think you might change your mind . . . you don't know how good it could be" (p. 62). In the student and leader manuals of *A.C. Green's Game Plan* (Phelps & Gray, 2001), one student says to another, "You're still a virgin? You don't know what you're missing" (p. 75). In one AOUM curriculum where boys are warned of forward girls, girls tell one guy "we can just have a little fun" (*Aspire*, Phelps, 2006, p. 12). Thus, in these curricula, the acknowledgment that sex is pleasurable is put into the mouths of unreliable "players," trying to talk people into having sex. Clearly, having sex because it is pleasurable is considered not to be an adequate argument, and puts an adolescent at risk.

For AOUM curricula, pleasure is also connected to the danger of being out of control, as well as to shame and guilt. The authors of *Journey*, for example, imply that sex is addictive and that it takes "more sexual activity each time to get back to the same level of excitement" (Cook, 2006, p. 54). They also write that setting boundaries helps to protect someone from getting out of control. When students end up having sex by making a decision in "the heat of the moment," they also end up feeling upset and ultimately breaking up (Cook, 2006, p. 54). The *Game Plan* manuals (Phelps & Gray, 2001) note that students are sometimes surprised at the shame and guilt they may feel.

Another danger of sexual pleasure is written about in both AOUM and CSE curricula; this danger has to do with deviance. AOUM curricula warn students that the pleasure of pornography can lead to an addiction. In *Aspire* (Phelps, 2006), boys are warned against thinking of women as "just 'something' to have fun with" (p. 12). *Streetwise to Sexwise* (Brown & Taverner, 2001), a CSE curriculum, also warns that pleasurable feelings can become linked to sexually exploitative behavior and that some youths can develop deviant sexual interests because of this association.

It is important to remember that AOUM curricula were strongly supported when comprehensive programs, like *Streetwise to Sexwise*, were written and ultimately may have influenced CSE authors' presentation of pleasure discourse. Thus even in comprehensive curricula, when pleasure is mentioned, the pleasure of sex is depicted as something that leads the student down a dangerous road toward intercourse or toward intercourse without proper protection. In *Making Sense of Abstinence*, having oral sex undermines Maria and her boyfriend's resolve to be abstinent because *he* gets excited and wants to do more. In this same curriculum, students are presented with a male character who states, "I am so hot. It feels so right and so good" and are subsequently asked to devise a response that could express the character's resolve to remain abstinent (Taverner & Montfort, 2005, p. 105). In *Reducing the Risk*, a CSE/EB curriculum, the authors acknowledge in one scenario that "you begin kissing and touching and feeling really good." This acknowledgment, however, is immediately followed by text encouraging the student to refuse a boyfriend or girlfriend who wants to have sex (practicing how to say no is also included) (Barth, 2004, pp. 58–59).

In spite of these examples, which invariably seem outdated and out of touch, in the 21st century, CSE curricula have made major gains in the discussion of pleasure. For example, comprehensive curricula authors write of pleasure in their discussions of protection during intercourse. They obviously are working with the belief that condoms reduce pleasure as a major obstacle to adolescents using them. In *Reducing the Risk*, a "doubt" expressed is "it won't feel as good if we use a condom" but a "doubt-buster" is "be sure we don't rush so we can enjoy the whole time together before, during and after the condom" (p. 192). In this curriculum the enhancement of pleasure is used as a way to ensure condom use. In other curricula, students are asked to respond with reasons to "scripts" in which guys say "It's like taking a shower with a raincoat on" (Goldfarb & Casparian, 2000), and "It's going to spoil it if we have to stop and put on a condom" (Barth, 2004, p. 193).

Other curricula call the pleasuring of someone else without intercourse "outercourse," and use the words "pleasure" and "desire" readily (e.g., *Positive Images*, Brick & Taverner, 2001, and *Streetwise to Sexwise*, Brown & Taverner, 2001). Intending to remain gender neutral, the authors of these curricula treat individuals of different genders similarly without direct information about what might be pleasurable or more pleasurable for adolescent girls. *Making Sense of Abstinence* discusses what can make a person "horny" (Taverner & Montfort, 2005). And *Our Whole Lives* (Goldfarb & Casparian, 2000), though not a school-based curriculum, writes of sensuality as "accepting and enjoying your own body and its ability to respond sexually as well as enjoying the body of a sexual partner" (p. 136).

AOUM curricula do not avoid talking about pleasure, but the authors of them use the promise of pleasure without guilt and worry as the reward for abstinence when a student finally has intercourse in heterosexual marriage. For example, *Game Plan* talks about sex being like a fire that is beautiful and gives warmth to the home, but "outside the fireplace, it can cause serious harm" (Phelps & Gray, 2001, p. 11).

GENDER STEREOTYPES CONTINUE TO BE A PROBLEM

A series of critiques have addressed the biological determinism in sex education curricula (Schwartz, 2005; Whatley, 1986, 1987, 1988, 1989). These critiques examined how curricula emphasized the role that testosterone plays in male sex drive to support a view of male sexual drive as powerful and unstoppable. Whatley (1988) described this discourse in AOUM curricula of a "powerful, innate, hormonally determined sex drive in men, with very little indication that there might be some equivalent in women" (p. 104). These ideas not only show boys and men to be powerful, but also subjects or agents of their own sexuality, an agency that is contrasted with female passivity (Holland et al., 1998). In this way, the curricula reinforce the double standard of sexual behavior (Whatley, 1987). Others have noted that men are represented as constantly on the lookout for sex and interested in having it whenever and wherever they can get it (Allen, 2004; Lamb, 1997; Trudell, 1992). In this way, excessive male desire is naturalized (Bay-Cheng, 2003). There are very few representations of positive male sexuality (Ashcraft, 2006).

One example of this naturalization of hypersexual males comes from the *Sex Respect* curriculum in which Dr. Wise, a character in the curriculum, says that girls fail to realize that boys get more turned on in the early phases of sexual play than girls do and that this can lead to sexual assault. Dr. Wise goes on to say he has counseled "dozens of young men who have beaten or raped girls. In every case, the male's excuse was that 'she led me on.' Ignorance of the steps of intimacy can have serious, even fatal, consequences" (Mast, 1986, p. 5). Not only is this example an egregious case of blaming the victim for her own assault, but it pictures all boys as potential rapists whose aggression is driven by their powerful sexual feelings in the early steps of intimacy. Within many AOUM curricula, girls are pictured as sexual gatekeepers who do not have sex for pleasure (Lamb, Graling, & Lustig, 2011; Schwartz, 2005).

WAIT (Why Am I Tempted?) Training (Krauth, 2003) includes a discussion of gender differences, stating up front that its goal is to celebrate difference, but including stereotypes such as, "Men are like microwaves; women are like crockpots" (Krauth, 2003, p. 184). In addition, a story of two dogs, Fido and Fifi, teaches about instinct and choices. Fido is strong and handsome. Fifi is a poodle with fluffy fur, wearing a rhinestone collar, nail polish, and perfume, and obviously is a nice choice for Fido, who is about to make a move on her. But then along comes another dog in heat. She is "mangy, toothless, smelly, flea-infested, and homeless," and yet Fido jumps on her. The explanation for this behavior is because he is ruled by his "bottom," called "command central," and he can't help but want to have sex with the dog who's available (Krauth, 2003, pp. 63–64). The moral is that humans have choices and don't have to have sex with any mangy, toothless person in heat who comes along. The stereotypes are clear. Respectable women take care of themselves, and here, taking care of themselves means making themselves pretty. Moreover, boys are uncontrollable, and so they might be tempted by any "slut" who comes by. They should wait for the more attractive (and richer) girl.

In another curriculum activity, a girlfriend with whom a boy has had sex is represented by transparent packing tape. The instructor says, "This is your girlfriend. She is kind of thin and transparent" (Krauth, 2003, p. 151). The teacher then wraps the tape around the boy's bare arms, over and over again, representing that they have had sex. When they break up, he tries to pull the tape off, but a bit of his DNA goes with it. Students are told to take a look at the tape, and look how hard it was to pull her off. This represents "Oxytocin—Love's Crazy Glue" (p. 151).

Later in the curriculum, students learn the different needs of men and women. They are told that women need caring, understanding, respect, devotion, and validation. Men need trust, acceptance, appreciation, and admiration (Krauth, 2003, p. 196). And men do not need validation? Respect? Women do not need appreciation? Admiration?

One major critique of sex education has been that it has focused too much on danger instead of desire (Fields, 2005; Fine, 1988; Kendall, 2008a; Schwartz, 2005). The overarching message of sexuality curricula continues to be that sexuality makes girls vulnerable to victimization (Froyum, 2009). If men have little control over their sexuality (biology stereotype), and women are vulnerable to their advances (danger stereotype), then girls need to be taught to prevent their own victimization and to screen possible rapists and potential dates (Schwartz, 2005). This reproduces a rhetoric of male entitlement (Froyum, 2009) that supports men as pursuers and women as pursued, or in other words, boys as sexual aggressors and girls as sexual avoiders (Fields, 2005; Froyum, 2009; Rose, 2005). Thus, sexuality curricula teach "refusal skills" for two important reasons—to avoid abuse and to avoid intercourse. Fields (2008) observed during her research that in one sex education class, girls were given "assertive refusal" exercises whereas boys were taught how to politely break up with a girl. In this case, the role plays assigned to girls the role of object and to boys the role of aggressor. She explains that when this happens, girls are made responsible for abstinence, their own and boys'.

In addition to their emphasis on young women's gatekeeper role, scripts for adolescent women emphasize passivity and objectification (Holland et al., 1998). Objectification refers to the reduction of women to their bodies, body parts, or body functions that exist for the use and pleasure of others (Fredrickson & Roberts, 1997). Critics have pointed out that sex education rarely acknowledges that girls can have sexual feelings (Fine, 1988; Whatley, 1987). For Black, low-income girls, exploring or expressing desire makes them further vulnerable to the stereotype of being a "ho" (Froyum, 2009). Fine writes that "A genuine discourse of desire would invite adolescents to explore what feels good and bad, desirable and undesirable, grounded in experiences, needs, and limits" (1988, p. 33). She claims that naming "desire" for girls is akin to permitting girls entitlement to a range of sexual feelings. Without sexual entitlement, Fine (1988) argues, girls are more vulnerable to sexual victimization and teen pregnancy. Similarly, Allen (2004) argues that teaching desire to girls (or permitting discussion of desire in the curriculum) combats the widespread objectification of girls and their tendency to to see themselves only as sexual objects for boys' pleasure.

However, Lamb, Graling, and Lustig (2011) found in their analysis of four AOUM curricula that were used between 2000 and 2010 that within these curricula, girls are depicted differently. They are presented as fully agentic beings capable of choice, a choice that the curricula authors want to influence. Although they describe circumstances that interfere with girls' agency (e.g., having been victimized in the past, being pressured into sex), in the end, the emphasis on choice in these curricula results in writing that appears to foster girls' sexual agency, telling girls they are capable of choosing abstinence, before and even after having had sex.

Lamb et al. (2011) also noted in these curricula what might seem like progress, in that there were examples of girls pressuring boys to have sex almost as frequently as boys pressuring girls. These examples represent the undoing of the former stereotype of women as purely passive and men as the purely active pursuer. Two of the curricula analyzed presented vignettes of manipulative girls with hapless teen boys. In one, a pregnant teen attempts to have sexual intercourse with a boy in order to trick him into believing he is the father of the baby. Still, this girl is not *really* portrayed as having sexual desire. Instead she is portrayed as a temptress who uses her sexuality to get what she wants from men. The presentation of women in this manner reflects hostile sexism. Hostile sexism involves the perception of women as not fully competent, lacking the necessary traits to hold positions of power, and as manipulators who use their sexual charms to lure men (Glick & Fiske, 1996). This type of attitude has been linked to prejudice and is reflected in negative and hostile attitudes toward women (Travaglia, Overall, & Sibley, 2009).

So, while girls are now portrayed as more agentic, do AOUM curricula also see them as more desiring? In short, yes, but this is a problematic desire and not positive in any way. In several vignettes or testimonials, girls were presented as so sexually aggressive that they were "daring" each other to try to get to a boy. The implication here is that a boy who is resolved to be abstinent must be prepared to withstand strong temptation. Thus, girls can be "bad" girls by being manipulative temptresses or daring "girls gone wild."

Despite the fact that girls seem to be agentic, desiring beings, problems remain. Philosopher Lawrence Blum, writing on racism, speaks of a "false symmetry" when a particular problematic behavior "is assumed to carry the same moral significance when its target is Whites as when it is Blacks" (forthcoming, p. 1). For example, asking a White person to sit at the back of the bus can never have the same moral significance as asking a Black person to do so, considering all the history and context of that act. Apply that to AOUM curricula and a different kind of false symmetry is set up: that girls are pressuring boys to have sex and that this is incredibly problematic. Curricula offered some acknowledgment that boys pressure girls much more frequently than the other way around, but presenting these extreme versions of female manipulation—girls using hard-to-resist sexuality—gives the *impression* of a symmetry that most likely does not exist. When girls and boys are treated equally it undermines an awareness of context and consequences that might be different for boys and girls as a result of the pressure. One of these is the greater risk for girls of non-consensual sex.

TEACHING APPROACHES MISS THE MARK

Other criticisms have more to do with how the curricula are taught than with the curricula themselves. Kehily (2002) writes that teachers sometimes do not follow the curricula very well and that the position of teachers *vis-à-vis* students in terms of power may shape the curricula in problematic ways. Kehily (2002) writes that many have asked for more informal methods, but these informal strategies often lead teachers to expect that students will open up in discussion and confide in them. Kehily (2002) states that low-income students do not respond positively to such expectations. Thomson and Scott (1991) noted that students would use sex education classes as social events and their own sexual knowledge to challenge and embarrass teachers. Teachers complain that students giggle and make jokes and can't handle the information (Ashcraft, 2006; Finders, 1999). In this way, education can establish an us-versus-them relationship, wherein teachers are the mature, responsible adults who find themselves positioned against irresponsible teens (Ashcraft, p. 2150).

Kehily also notes the disjunction between school and "the world of popular culture" (2002, p. 217). As Brown, Halpern, and L'Engle (2005) state, the media has become a "sexual super peer" in its ability to educate and influence adolescents about sexuality. Thus, it seems important that any sex education curriculum would take into account popular culture, and the sex education it provides to students.

Kehily notes in her qualitative study that the approach taken by a teacher, a teacher she describes as having credibility with low-income youths, who himself wasn't necessarily a "goody goody" back in the day, was the most effective approach to getting students to talk: "You're not going to shock me by the things that you do because I've done it all and worse . . ." (2002, p. 223). And although the teacher was in some way understood to be exploiting his masculine privilege, both girls and boys in the school sought him out for discussion and confessions. Brown, Lamb, and Tappan (2009) note that those men who do masculinity studies and frequently present talks in high schools often start out their talks with masculine credentials. For example, one may begin a lecture by saying he was a football player. And while he then goes on to talk about the hidden vulnerabilities of the jock and all boys, it appears that he first must establish himself as a "regular guy" in order to do so. One wonders whether this strategy might work for sex education classes, too, or whether it is a particularly gendered approach. The former "player" and "bad boy" would seem to have more credibility in the classroom than the former "slut" but perhaps not the single mom who regrets the adolescence she never had.

Baber and Murray (2001) discuss the qualities of a feminist classroom as achieving participation through openness and the promotion of quality, trust, and respect for differences. They write that such an approach (one that emphasizes respect) can be inclusive when there are students from various religious and political backgrounds in the same class. Personal narrative and the inclusion of relationships also make their approach feminist. Allowing personal narrative, they claim, gives space for students to make sense of their lives and sexual development in an integrative way. They also advocate for action projects such that students may work together to encourage change, for example, preparing brochures on sexual issues and distributing them or planning and implementing a bisexual support group. They suggest that the instructors model being a change agent and talk about his or her own activities to incite change.

Interviews with sex educators show that they self-censor because of discomfort with explicit material (Harrison, Hillier, & Walsh, 1996). Research suggests that some content area is "risky" and that teachers may prefer the relationship questions to the explicit questions regarding sex acts. Teachers also indicated that they worry about crossing boundaries in the classroom and getting negative feedback from parents. They might address this by making themselves more formal or even inaccessible. One teacher Harrison and colleagues interviewed remarked that she felt protected because she was married (Harrison et al., 1996).

As noted in this chapter's section on health-focused curricula as well as in this section on teaching, manual-based or standardized sex education benefits teachers; it enables them to talk freely about subjects that they are uncomfortable teaching. However, it also hinders their efforts; it confines teachers to the material presented in the book. Moreover, students are restricted to a "workbooky" kind of education, with simplistic lessons and fill-in-the-blank self-tests on facts. However, manualized sex education is important when the case is made for use of only *effective* curriculum. In the war against AOUM curricula, this has been an important case to make.

HEALTH IS A FOCUS AT THE EXPENSE OF OTHER ISSUES

In examining most of the curricula that were developed to compete against AOUM curricula because of their effectiveness, the appeal of sex education's public health focus is readily apparent. Sexual health is important and affects more than just the individual student, especially in terms of preventing pregnancy and the spread of STIs. Poor sex education in the late 20th and early 21st centuries has put adolescents at risk for pregnancy and STIs: "The bottom line is that abstinence-only approaches deny youth access to important health information, and evidence suggests that students in these programs are more likely to engage in unsafe sex than students in comprehensive programs" (Boonstra, 2004, as cited in Ashcraft, 2006, p. 2153).

The health issues are so important that I have been one of the only critics of late to argue that such a narrow focus poses a number of potential problems. In a 2010 piece, I argued that focusing on health leaves out other important dimensions of sexual experience and sexual development that young people need. Moreover, I argued that a focus on health sets up curricula for facts-based learning that appears to have no moral dimension with regard to how students might behave with one another. Finally, I noted that the health focus led to manualized education and testable outcomes. This kind of sex education depends on social skills training, a kind of education that focuses on practice rather than understanding, and that practice leads to better choices. This makes sense to an extent. The student who practices going to buy condoms at a store will certainly feel more at ease while buying them in the future. The student who practices ten different ways to say no will most likely feel he or she has a way to say no should he or she want to. But such an indication relates very specifically to abstinence and health choices, failing to address a range of other worrisome issues concerning sex and students. These curricula don't address the need for thinking and processing feelings and understandings about how we practice sex in society, and the implications for both individuals and society.

Ashcraft (2006) is another critic who raises questions regarding the effectiveness of the current approach. She writes that "the problem with sex education is not so much that it is 'ineffective,' but rather that the very language of 'effectiveness' cloaks important power dynamics and naturalizes certain strategies for approaching teen sexuality" (p. 2149). She argues that because of the emphasis on effectiveness, information can focus on biological topics that are presumed to be neutral while masking all sorts of universal rules of behavior, independent of context and insensitive to gender, race, class, and sexual orientation.

Thus, effectiveness (and health) cannot be the only measure of a good sex education. Health education needs to make room for something bigger, broader, and more idealistic for developing students.

CURRICULA ARE INEFFECTIVE

One of the major criticisms proffered by those who advocate for comprehensive sexuality curricula has been that AOUM curricula are ineffective. Kirby (2001) reviewed 73 curricula that had been tested and found that there were only three studies of AOUM curricula—only one met the criteria for inclusion in the meta-analysis based on the requirement of a solid methodology. The study could only conclude whether CSE curricula were effective given the paucity of information on AOUM curricula.

Congress also became involved in assessing the effectiveness of curricula. Its efforts at assessment appear in the form of the Waxman Report (2004). The authors of this report reviewed 13 school-based curricula that were being used in all regions of the United States, and found that 80% of them contained "false, misleading, or distorted information about reproductive health" (2004, p. i). The extent to which curricula were accurate in their presentation of information, however, did not exactly constitute a test of efficacy. One might suppose that if telling lies to high schoolers was effective in preventing pregnancy and STIs, there might be some support for that program.

The National Campaign to Prevent Teen and Unplanned Pregnancy supported another study by Douglas Kirby (2007) to assess the effectiveness of programs. In the time since Kirby's 2001 report, Kirby noted the number of studies measuring program impact increased substantially, and the methodologies used also improved. About two-thirds of curriculum-based sex and STI/HIV education programs had some positive effect on teen sexual behavior. The author found no strong evidence that any abstinence program delayed the initiation of sex, hastened the return to abstinence, or reduced the number of sexual partners. Not many studies evaluated the effectiveness of AOUM programs, but those that existed showed that they didn't have a *negative* impact on the use of condoms or other contraceptives. In general, however, there simply wasn't enough evidence to support using them. In contrast, out of 48 programs that supported both abstinence and the use of contraceptives (including condoms) for sexually active teens, two-thirds were effective in changing teen behavior. It is important to note that no comprehensive program caused teens to start having sex earlier, nor did CSE curricula increase the frequency with which teens were having sex. These kinds of programs were effective for both genders, all major ethnic groups, and experienced and inexperienced teens, independent of community. Almost all of the comprehensive programs had an effect on factors that influence behavior, such as the attitudes and intentions of teens.

Another report with seemingly opposite conclusions was also released in 2007. The report was commissioned by the Agency for Children and Families (ACF) in the Department of Health and Human Services in response to the Waxman Report, at the request of two Republican abstinence supporters, Senator Rick Santorum and Senator Tom Coburn. The ACF contracted with the conservative Sagamore Institute for Policy Research, according to a Guttmacher report (Guttmacher Institute, 2007). Some of the confusing material in this report is as follows. The authors say they examined nine curricula that were supported with federal money, but they examined CSE and EB curricula during a period in which no CSE curriculum was supported with federal funding. They counted words as a method of determining how much attention was being paid to topics. So they counted the number of times words relating to contraception were used. However, they only counted the words *abstinence* and *abstain* rather than related words such as *avoid*, *delay*, or *wait*. They also claimed there was medically inaccurate information, but the examples were minor, such as the use of the term *dental dam* instead of *rubber dam*, or that one curriculum stated all condoms marketed in the United States meet federal standards. They purposely distort, for example, a "red light/green light" exercise regarding HIV risk to mean that the CSE authors were saying showering together is a "no risk" activity when they gave it a green light. The authors obviously were making a point that showering was not risky for HIV infection or pregnancy; however, if showering together led to unprotected intercourse, it might indeed be risky. They go on to present behaviors such as having unprotected intercourse in the "red light" column. The Guttmacher Institute criticizes the report for not comparing the curricula on effectiveness. No matter how many times the word *abstinence* is mentioned in a CSE curriculum (as if the mere mention of the word somehow increases the reader's will to remain abstinent), the CSE curricula the report examined were more effective than AOUM curricula in delaying first sex and increasing condom use.

That same year, a long-term study of four AOUM programs was finally published (Trenholm et al., 2007). This study was conducted by Mathematica Policy Research on behalf of the U.S. Department of Health and Human Services, and the researchers did not find evidence that AOUM programs were effective in increasing abstinence. They did find that friends' support for abstinence predicts future abstinence, but that this support of abstinence drops dramatically from middle school to high school years. This study also showed that over the 4 years of the study, the typical youth who had five close friends during year 1 only had two close friends who still supported abstinence later on.

Another study of interest with regard to the curriculum that I propose later in this book is one that was commissioned by the National Campaign to Prevent Teen Pregnancy. This study reported that teens cite moral and religious beliefs as significant factors in their decision to not engage in sex. The survey (Kirby, 2001) found that "religious" young people are more likely to delay having sex, and that a message emphasizing particular traditional and religious values can be powerful and positive. Thus, if delaying sex has positive outcomes for teens, and sex education wants to help promote this delay, encouraging students to examine and discuss their religious beliefs with their parents, as well as in school, may be fruitful. However, in the current climate, religion is often kept out of CSE curricula and has been associated only with the AOUM forms of sex education. This may be an issue that CSE curricula authors want to reappraise.

CURRICULA LACK AN EXPLICIT MORAL PERSPECTIVE

While AOUM curricula tend to promote morals such as respect for self and others, responsibility, self-discipline, self-control, integrity, honesty, fairness, and kindness (Krauth, 2003, p. 18), health-oriented comprehensive curricula tend to be less explicit. Even the SIECUS statement about guidelines for middle school sex education, "Values should be freely chosen after the alternatives and their consequences are evaluated" (p. 18), feels morally weak. The difference in the treatment of moral issues comes from the fact that comprehensive sex education advocates have overinvested in science and health to the exclusion of core values and morals most schools and parents would like their teens to develop and apply to their sexual lives.

This is not to say that AOUM curricula do a wonderful job at presenting universal values to the students they educate. For example, when AOUM curricula talk about mutuality and intimacy, they are not citing these as aspects of "good sex," but using these qualities as a way to advocate for sex in marriage. Strangely, current curricula say very little regarding the other person, that is, the person with whom one may be engaging in sex. With the heavy emphasis on health information and health care in sex ed, one might forget that sex typically involves two people. Sadly, intimacy in and of itself isn't valued. Sometimes it even appears in various curricula as something that interferes with decision making and not only as something positive that adults want students to express and have in their relationships. In one curriculum, *Reducing the Risk*, a CSE-supported and EB curriculum, love and infatuation are shown to lead to self-deception. Arousal is discussed only as a physical sensation and not as something that may go hand in hand with feeling close to and then desirous of another person. In an abstinence-based curriculum written by comprehensive sex ed advocates, *Making Sense of Abstinence*, intimacy is discussed as part of a unit about oral sex, the implication being that oral sex is less intimate an act and that students need to consider this. *Reducing the Risk* shows relationship building as an alternative to having sex and ask students in the unit on "Refusals" to consider how teenagers "should" show affection to someone they love. In these curricula, as in the AOUM curriculum, feeling close and "a lot of touching" can lead to a "crisis" in which a student may not be able to protect her- or himself before having sex.

Mutuality and intimacy may not exactly be moral goals, but empathy, caring, and the ability to take another's perspective into account are virtues in moral education, so one would expect these qualities to appear more frequently than they do in sex ed curricula. Instead, autonomy and self-reflection are promoted as integral components of the pathway toward decision making. Making a decision together or understanding how the other person feels or thinks is depicted as an action that interferes with self-care or taking one's own aims seriously. Again, in *Making Sense of Abstinence*, where students are asked to "to find out how the other person feels" and to talk honestly and listen carefully, one might think that the other person is being considered with empathy and care. But then the student is urged to "stand up for your decision" (p. 104) as if the other person is only there as an obstacle to the student's resolve, and not as a living, breathing other that he or she might care about. Missing also is the idea that a student might be influenced by what someone else says or wants and that a decision might be made mutually. In *Reducing the Risk*, in a discussion of how to build the relationship as an alternative to not having sex or as a delaying tactic, a person who has just refused sex can say to the other, "I know this isn't easy for you" (p. 85). The curriculum presents a list of refusal strategies like turning away, ending the situation, and saying "I've got to go now" (p. 85), but the moving "I know this isn't easy for you" stands out as one that reflects a real relationship in a sea of "I" statements—"I feel/think/want/don't want, so you must do X."

Another ethical focus is noticeably absent from sex education curricula—that is, the moral injunction to not harm others. This ethic is the focus of anti-rape education, but why doesn't sex ed today also include anti-rape education? Moira Carmody (2005), in New Zealand, writes that so many courses regarding rape and sexual behavior are focused on young women and their choices, whereas courses that addresses young men's behavior are perhaps more crucial to the prevention of rape and unwanted sex. Carmody (2005) writes that we are failing to teach young people skills they need to negotiate pleasurable and ethical sexual intimacy and that a lack of negotiated consent is at the root of the problem. She calls for a major shift in sex education from refusal skills and awareness-raising to a focus on promoting and developing non-violent relating.

In addition to responding to the ethic of not harming someone else, curricula might do more to address what students' rights are and how students respect the rights of others. Some curricula hint at rights without stating them. For example, in the CSE curriculum *Reducing the Risk* (Barth, 2004) the authors state two rights that they claim are implicit values in the curriculum: "No one should feel pressured to engage in sexual activities. No one should pressure someone else to do something they do not wish to do sexually" (p. 218). *Making Sense of Abstinence* (Taverner & Montfort, 2005), one of my favorite groups of lessons, begins with a declaration of "fundamental rights" at the beginning of the curriculum, rights that emphasize the right to abstain: students should "understand that the option not to have sexual intercourse is a basic human *right* that an individual should be able to assert at any time in any relationship" (p. xiii, emphasis mine). They also indicate that students should know they have a right to make their own decisions in these areas, emphasizing autonomy in decision making.

It is interesting to note, however, that few if any curricula include information about laws that address students' autonomy and responsibility, where these laws derive from, how they are protected, and how these laws are relaxed or emphasized in matters of sex. Educating for citizenship in a democracy generally includes teaching about one's rights, so why not sexual rights? With no context provided about where these rights come from, they are in danger of being challenged or eliminated when governments change. Moreover, students may become passive in relation to their rights and less autonomous in their exercising of them. Such a discussion of rights need not only focus on whether a teen is free to make his or her own choices with regard to sex, but also what rights and protections are afforded him or her with regard to matters such as education, contraception, coercion, and privacy.

Lessons about fair and equal treatment of others with regard to sexual behavior, as well as lessons about respect, ought to accompany those that discuss treating others with care. Some curricula do discuss respect in units about gender equity and sexual orientation. That the language of respect and fairness is not deeply imbedded in what sex is and how to behave, but is brought up as a reminder around difference is deeply problematic.

CONCLUSION

Considered collectively, these critiques of sex education today present a sad picture. Curricula are riddled with stereotypes; tend to exclude LGBTQ youth; do not support democratic education; skirt around the idea of pleasure; show a White, middle-class, heterosexist bias; have been shown to be ineffective with regard to prevention of STIs, pregnancy, and first sex; and, perhaps most importantly, have lost their ethical focus. AOUM advocates accuse comprehensive sex education advocates of having a hidden curriculum that encourages sex before marriage. Comprehensive sex education advocates argue the not-so-hidden curriculum of the AOUM curricula ignores teen sexuality today and places them in danger of STIs and pregnancy. Their tactic of supporting evidence-based programs that prevent pregnancy and STIs was important in the fight for comprehensive sex ed, but it ceded talk of values to only the most conservative perspectives. Talk of values, morals, and ethics is and should be an important part of sex education, as will be discussed in Chapter 3.

CHAPTER 3

Toward a New Ethical Focus

There are core ethical values that are held, more or less, universally.
Virtually all societies share some fundamental ideas about what
constitutes good and evil. . . . Particularly at this time, when there
is such a crisis of character, when unethical behavior abounds, it
is most appropriate for schools to target these core ethical values
[respect for self and others, responsibility, self-discipline, self-control,
integrity, honesty, fairness, kindness, etc.] as objectives for curricular
development.

—Joneen Krauth, *WAIT Training*, 2003, p. 18

Ignoring the phrase about unethical behavior abounding today, there is
not much to disagree with in this quote from the AOUM curriculum *WAIT
(Why Am I Tempted?) Training* (Krauth, 2003). As noted in Chapter 2, with
regard to sex ed, we want students to learn respect for self and others,
responsibility, self-discipline, self-control, integrity, honesty, fairness, and
especially kindness. If all proponents of sex education can agree on these
traits as moral, then why do we need AOUM advocates to remind us of
these important virtues? And why does a call for moral behavior in the
realm of sex need to be placed within the framework of a moral panic
about today's "crisis of character"?

Is there really a crisis of character? Maybe not, but these ethics,
among others, are teachable and important to include in sex education.
Why can't or won't comprehensive sexuality curricula or evidence-based
curricula speak to values? In Chapter 1 I described the shift from teaching
about "family values" and the abandonment of a public moral voice in
favor of the voice of science and evidence. In making this shift, advocates
of a more comprehensive sex ed permitted AOUM advocates to have
the *only* voice regarding values. And that voice connected character with
abstinence, which is a poor and narrow view of what it might mean to be
a person of good character.

One might ask, why should sex ed include ethics at all (Lamb, 2010)?
But doesn't it already? No matter how much any one curriculum tries to
stick with "the facts of life," there is an ethic underlying that choice. This

may even qualify as the "hidden curriculum" (Giroux & Penna, 1983) of sex ed programs. As Halstead and Reiss (2003) write, "values permeate every aspect of sex education in schools" (p. 3). Depending on what perspective the curriculum advocates, there is a direct or indirect set of ethics that underlie it. I argue that AOUM curricula authors have managed to speak directly about ethics, whereas the CSE curricula authors couch their ethics in a discourse of evidence-based science. Even in a health-based curriculum, however, a set of discoverable moral perspectives exists.

Halstead and Reiss (2003), in their book on values in sex education, write that sex education is like every other subject in the curriculum except that it is about human relationships, and because it is about human relationships, it includes a central moral dimension. They argue that the selection of aims, content, and method all imply values, and that even the decision to promote sex education at all expresses a value. The transmission of values can also be indirectly conveyed by a teacher or a school.

Here are some basic ethical judgments that seem to underlie many sex ed enterprises, regardless of whether they originate from a CSE or AOUM perspective:

- Teens are not entirely autonomous and it is adults'/society's obligation to help them in the realm of sex (CSE and AOUM tend to agree on this).
- Sex in a relationship is more ethical than sex outside of a relationship (CSE generally agrees with AOUM advocates on this, although AOUM advocates will add that the only relationship in which sex is ethical is marriage).
- Choice and freedom must be preserved (surprisingly, AOUM and CSE advocates agree on this; the language about preserving one's freedom by not having sex and not getting pregnant at a young age abounds in AOUM curricula, and yet at times the restrictions of others' rights brings in a question about their sincerity).
- One has a responsibility to take care of oneself and treat one's body well (both agree here also).
- One shouldn't hurt other people (both AOUM and CSE advocates agree on this ethic).

One could argue that some of these statements are opinions that have no moral basis, for example, that sex in a relationship is more ethical than sex outside of a relationship. Few would argue with the statement that relationships are *good* for teens. Isolation in adolescence leads to myriad problems, and relationships help teens' self-esteem and ability to cope with problems, as well as increase their overall well-being. These positive outcomes, however, are not explicitly ethical reasons for promoting relationships. Many curricula subtly and not so subtly communicate the notion that it is better to have sex in a relationship than to have sex outside of a relationship for health reasons, *and* for moral reasons. Some AOUM curricula explicitly say that sex is more meaningful and precious in a relationship, specifically heterosexual marriage. Some comprehensive curricula also imply that sex is best or better when one cares about the other person. I will explore that and other moral claims, direct and indirect, in the rest of this chapter.

UNIVERSAL ETHICS

While in this book I tend to use the words *values* and *ethics* interchangeably, I prefer *ethics*. These are just words, but the word *values* suggests something akin to a personal preference. Ethics, instead, can refer to moral principles that people either use intentionally, through reason, or without much thought, implicitly, that guide their understanding and decision making regarding what is right and wrong, what is good and bad, what is demeaning and uplifting, worthy of respect or worthy of condemnation, fair and unfair, and caring and callous. And these ethics, I argue, are more or less universal.

Much has been written on universal ethics, that is, ethical principles that can be applied to all cultures, schools, and families. In this book, I attempt to focus primarily upon those specific ethics that appear to be universal and leave it to students in the classroom to argue about *relativism*, the belief that ethical judgments are based on wishes, desires, interests, attitudes, likes, and dislikes, all relative to an individual and his or her culture (Curtler, 2004). The judgment that it is wrong to rape a woman, for example, from a relativistic view, would be simply a matter of opinion, and although we punish people in our culture for this crime, we might go on to say that we can't judge whether it might be right or wrong in another culture. I maintain, however, that while rape might be treated differently in different cultures, that is, as more or less harmful or as a serious crime versus as an annoyance, it is wrong. And while there are circumstances that make people in a given culture think a rape is more or less deserved (as in American culture when undergraduates endorse items on a Rape Myth questionnaire that indicate that if a woman dresses a certain way or lets a man pay for her meal, she is more deserving of rape), rape is still wrong. So when I discuss ethics, I refer to more or less universal ethics as well as ethics that can be supported through a process of justification. These ethical principles, although universal, are indeed debatable, and I hope they will be recognized as such in the classroom so that students can learn how to justify their own moral beliefs in that context.

Human Rights and Justice

In examining the types of ethics underlying sex ed today, we can look specifically at what kinds of "rights" are afforded to adolescents. For the time being, let's put aside the fact that in the United States, adolescents do not have some rights because they aren't of legal age. Nonetheless, looking broadly at human rights, it is clear that human beings who live in societies have certain rights. This is a universal principle, although *which* human beings have them and *what kinds* of rights they have are hotly debated and change over time and in different circumstances. Several revolutions and civil wars around the globe have centered around the idea that *all* human beings have rights, including the right to self-determination. However, there are still slaves and groups of humans believed to be inferior or deserving of fewer rights in various cultures, including the United States.

That it is wrong to harm another human being seems to be a universal ethic, too. However, in war we harm; in fact, the nature or war mandates it. Even parents, by no means required to harm their children, hurt them when they spank them. Thus, while we might agree that this ethic of nonmaleficence is a universal ethic worth acknowledging, it is clear that the nuances of this ethic merit discussion.

There is a lack of consensus with regard to how universal ethical principles should be interpreted, what the important exceptions to them are, and what an ethical principle is exactly. Respect, fairness, and human happiness are ethics that arise from the Western tradition. Curtler (2004) summarizes them as follows:

1. Treat the person in yourself and others with respect.
2. Treat all persons fairly.
3. Consistent with 1 and 2, adopt a rule for action that will increase the happiness of a majority of those affected by the rule. (p. 44)

We might add to these principles ideas about obligation, duty, autonomy, justice, consent, and human rights. These ethics that suggest duties, principles, and rights are still within the justice framework encapsulated by the three principles above. Halstead and Reiss (2003) write that liberal values from the Western tradition are a group of intersecting positions but can be reduced to this set of values: freedom, equality, and rationality.

Implied in these three ideas are personal autonomy, state impartiality, individual respect, equal rights to freedom, and just resolution of conflict. Liberal ethicists disagree with regard to whether the consequences of acts or whether moral duties determine what is right or wrong. Halstead and Reiss (2003) write that liberal ethics as they are enacted in education mean education that values "personal autonomy, critical openness, equality of opportunity, rational morality, celebration of diversity, the avoidance of manipulation and indoctrination, the refusal to side with any particular definitive conception of the good, democratic values, citizenship, and children's rights" (p. 61).

Aristotelian Ethics

Aristotelian ethics speaks to a different set of ethics than those relating to rights and liberty. Instead this kind of ethics addresses virtues, rather than rights, and describes a moral or virtuous character. This strand of ethics conceptualizes education as a way of realizing potential virtues and learning to act in accordance with them through practice. This is different from the rights-based ethics described above, which emphasizes reasoning about or finding justifications for what's right and wrong.

Following Aristotle, philosophers such as Alasdair MacIntyre (1981) and Martha Nussbaum (2001) see ethics as stemming from obligations to others by virtue of our membership in families, communities, and societies. From this perspective, shared history and emotional attachment can guide the ethical practice of human beings as much as can the individualized or even disembodied rights and rules from the former tradition of justice and rights. For example, following Aristotelian tradition, an ethical decision maker may forfeit rights in favor of loyalty and belonging, and he or she must consider the particularity of the situation. In terms of sex education, some liberals' fear regarding "communitarian" values is that if people make judgments based on community or personal and particular values, we edge toward a relativism that may ultimately prevent us from saying what's right for anyone else.

Ethic of Care

There is another line of thinking in the field of ethics that seems close to this latter Aristotelian strand called the "caring" perspective. It hearkens back to David Hume, who thought that human beings' capacity for sympathy formed the basis of a natural morality. Carol Gilligan in the field of psychology (1982) and Nel Noddings (2002) in the field of education each put forward the idea that certain people tend to act from an ethic of care, prioritizing care over justice, and that this is a valid motivation for ethical behavior because the justice perspective doesn't take into consideration personal obligations and feelings toward others, both important parts of human relationships. This ethic of care has also been associated with groups that have less power, suggesting that those with power prefer a rights-based morality, given that legal systems are constructed in a way that advantages those with power, whereas an ethic of care mandates the principle, or the demand, that everyone be cared for and that no one should be harmed. Within this chapter and in Chapters 4 and 5, when talking about the curriculum, I refer to this ethic of care.

ETHICAL EDUCATION IN THE SEX ED CLASSROOM

I make two points about ethics and sex education that are fundamentally at variance with current comprehensive sex education enterprises. The first is that we absolutely need a sex ed course for teens that incorporates ethics; the second is that certain ethics should be taught and taught in the tradition of philosophical education. It is my hope that this book addresses the first point. Regarding the second point, although the teaching methods of the 1960s and the FLSE classroom gave students space and time to discuss and come up with their own points of view, which is important for adolescents' development, it would be wrong to return to the days where students simply came up with their own set of ethics. Their developmental stage may too likely influence a set of ethics that is inadequate to the task of meeting up with people sexually. For example, adolescents tend to want to be nonjudgmental, to "live and let live," or advocate that everyone should "do their own thing," but this is not an adequate ethical stance for negotiating sexual interactions.

Given the increased demand for evidence-based programs, CSE and EB curricula use scientific data to support the values they present. Even the authors of AOUM curricula do not avoid data. They too find data and statistics to support their belief that students should remain abstinent. In the world of moral education, however, one doesn't teach ethical behavior by giving students scientific reasons to be ethical, for example, by telling them that if they are ethical, they will have fewer negative consequences or be hurt less. In the world of moral education, we teach students to do the right thing and to recognize what is the right thing to do through reasoned reflection.

I do not want to underestimate how important the scientific evaluations are, those that test whether a given curriculum is effective in delaying first sex and preventing STIs and unwanted teen pregnancies.

Outcome evaluations have not shown positive long-term effects of federally funded AOUM programs (Cagampang, Barth, Korpi, & Kirby, 1997;
Kirby, 2001, 2002, 2007; LeCroy & Milligan Associates, 2003; Manlove,
Romano-Papillo, & Ikramullah, 2004; Trenholm et al., 2007). Also, Brückner and Bearman (2005), evaluating the effectiveness of virginity pledges,
found that although those who pledged were more likely to delay initiation of intercourse, 18 months after they pledged they were less likely to
have used contraception after they initiated sexual intercourse. At 6-year
follow-up, the prevalence of STIs in the pledging group was similar to
that among the non-pledgers and 88% had had sexual intercourse before
marriage (99% in the nonpledging group).

But these data do not answer the question of whether or not one
should teach abstinence or encourage virginity pledges. The data simply
show that the way these values are promoted today may cause more
harm than good. Still, EB and CSE advocates argue that AOUM curricula reflect poor values, while AOUM advocates level the same criticism
toward those who promote EB and CSE curricula in the schools.

The critics of the AOUM sex education agenda both imply and state
values that ought to be reflected in the policies of sex education as well
as in the curricula themselves. These values are standard liberal values,
many of which overlap, and are concerned with autonomy, non-discrim-
ination (or, equality), not reducing human beings to consumers (making
them a means to an end), inclusion (in terms of representation), freedom
to choose (as opposed to coercion), and instrumental values (for example,
it is better for teens to not have an STI, unwanted pregnancy, or sex at too
young an age). The feminist contribution to criticism of sex education has
focused specifically on its meaning to and consequences for girls, and yet
this criticism has implications for a general sex education policy.

AOUM critics claim that CSE curricula can be value-less or interfere
with parents' values, or, more specifically, "family values." They present
the ethical viewpoint that a parent has the right to choose what information his or her child receives, the values education a child receives, and
the timing and nature of that education. While this right of a parent isn't
argued on behalf of a number of subjects taught in schools where curricula is determined by superintendents and school boards, they argue
that because sex is more values-based and personal than other topics, a
school's interference with a parent's right in this area is more problematic.

The AOUM curriculum *WAIT Training* addresses five aspects of students' sexual development: physical, intellectual, emotional, social, and
spiritual. Why can't comprehensive sex educators address these same fac-
ets of development? Why has "comprehensive" come to narrowly mean
"comprehensive with regard to contraception"? Why is the curriculum

Our Whole Lives taught in church basements and not in schools? Because, clearly, only one side of this debate is permitted to have values.

AOUM curricula use important values like respecting others and equal treatment to promote abstinence, ignoring how their lack of inclusiveness is disrespectful to some students. CSE curricula rarely discuss the treatment of the other person in sex, because if they did, they would need to take into consideration the other person in all his or her particularity, introducing a wide range of people, sexualities, and practices. Thus the only ethical perspective that CSE advocates have permission to convey is a vague injunction that if students use protection and know the facts of sex, moral behavior will follow.

The problem that exists for sex ed today is that those who advocate CSE have their hands tied. They've been pushed into a corner of presenting the most value-free, scientific, reduced curriculum that can't be attacked. On the other hand, the AOUM teachers are free to be as value-focused as they want to be.

In Chapters 4, 5, and 6, I imagine what an ethics-based curriculum might look like, the topics that might be covered, the moral issues that adhere, and the readings that would support a deep conversation of such. The curriculum does not promote abstinence only and indeed, doesn't even focus primarily on the question of whether to have sexual intercourse or not. Research tells us that students, when posed with thinking and reasoning that is slightly above their current reasoning ability, that asks them to integrate a speaker's views, or that presents some conflict for them to work through, improve their thinking and reason more clearly and with more complexity (Berkowitz & Gibbs, 1983; Blatt & Kohlberg, 1975). This curriculum aims to teach in this tradition.

There is a big, beautiful, confusing, scary, fascinating, and troubling world of sexuality all around teens today, so why not de-emphasize the "big decision" and leave that to advice columnists, peers, parents, and television shows, and instead help students to examine sexual behavior from an ethical perspective? In addition to the health information they receive elsewhere, and the religious education they receive at home, moral education can deeply affect a student's way of feeling and thinking about sex. This should influence behavior, encouraging students to behave ethically toward others and to develop strong and ethical views about sexual events and issues in the world around them.

CHAPTER 4

Sex Ed as Democratic Citizenship Education

This book was written for pre-service teachers who may or may not ever have the chance to teach a sex ed class. But if a student is training to teach English or social studies, or even philosophy, at the high school level, he or she could develop a course on sexual ethics, and I encourage him or her to do so even if he or she has little knowledge of sexual health. Even if there is no opportunity for the individual teacher to develop such a course, borrowing from our own SECS-C (Sex Education for a Caring Society Curriculum, Lamb et al., 2012), the new teacher can be an advocate in the school system with regard to the *kind* of sex education that is necessary to produce sexual citizens in our democracy.

It is not a new idea that education should produce democratic citizens. What is more or less new is that sex education should also serve this purpose. Amy Gutmann (1987), the author of *Democratic Education*, writes that democratic education encourages a student to develop a "deliberative character" (p. 52) as well as "widespread and enduring tolerance for different ways of life" (p. 54). Is that not a principle that should be applied to sex ed curricula? The father of democratic education, John Dewey (1909), saw the student as an eventual "member of a family, himself responsible . . . in turn, for rearing and training of future children, and thus maintaining the continuity of society" and who contributes to the "decencies and graces of civilization" (p. 10). Can't this philosophy guide a student's growth through sex ed? Philosopher Nel Noddings writes of Dewey's warning against "the isolation of formal citizenship from 'the whole system of relations with which it is actually interwoven'" (Noddings, 2002, p. 75). In other words, Dewey argued that citizenship can't be separated from the particularities of the lives students lead. And thus, sex ed curricula must not focus primarily on the individual student's health and decision making, but on his or her participation in a culture in which sex is had, seen, experienced, and represented.

Those who write about democratic education give several guiding principles. For example, democratic education must be non-restrictive.

That is, students must have the freedom to pursue their interests and ideas in the classroom as they are led in a variety of directions. Second, it must be non-dogmatic, which is not the same as free from values. Students should be presented with opportunities to reason and reflect on ideas and values, forming their own justifications of their beliefs and perspectives from a rational and emotional point of view. Third, a democratic education must be inclusive and proactive in its attempts to address inequalities and stereotypes, especially to include minority groups. Fourth, a democratic education ought to be dedicated to teaching deliberation over and critique of ideas and practices and tied to a process that is akin to shared governance, free from domination.

In keeping with democratic goals that sustain an attitude of caring, a sexual ethics curriculum ought to create an inclusive classroom, exploring rights and discussing sex and sexuality from the perspective of *community*, not just the rights of individual students who happen to identify as LGBTQ. When the curriculum includes lessons on gender stereotypes, sexual orientation, and discrimination, it should purposively cultivate ethical and equal treatment of others outside of the classroom and not only all students within.

A democratic sex ed needs to do more than teach students that discrimination and stereotyping are wrong because they are against the law or inaccurate. A discussion of the harm done to individuals and societies by discrimination is crucial for the development of a deeper understanding and commitment to work against it. And a discussion of the harm of gender stereotypes is deeply connected to sexual attitudes and behaviors that students will convey as they go out into the world. As Gutmann writes (1987, pp. 32–33), "Teaching mutual respect is instrumental to assuring all children the freedom to choose in the future . . . [S]ocial diversity enriches our lives by expanding our understanding of differing ways of life. To reap the benefits of social diversity, children must be exposed to ways of life different from their parents and—in the course of their exposure—must embrace certain values, such as mutual respect among persons . . ."

This chapter provides guidelines for implementing an ethical and democratic sex ed curriculum.

GET PERMISSION

A school will need to approve such a course, but investment from parents is also essential. No course at school makes parents more uncomfortable than a course on sex. Nonetheless, the vast majority of parents want their

children to discuss the sex that they see all around them and are sometimes at a loss with regard to how to convey their own values to their kids
with regard to this. Most parents will be pleased to hear that the SECS-C
includes discussions of media and even pornography. Parents are worried
about these things and the course initiates conversations that can be continued at home. One of the most important things to convey to parents is
that what they hear about the curriculum, in tidbits here and there, might
not always be entirely accurate. Ask them to be wary of what they hear
from their children and other parents, and give them full access to the
curriculum online and on paper so that they can peruse it and evaluate
it for themselves.

MAKE IT DEMOCRATIC, MAKE IT CARING

As Noddings (2002) also notes, Dewey proposed that in democratic education, the child has powers of self-direction, administration, and responsibility. Thus, lessons from the field of moral education would argue for a
classroom atmosphere that is built on jointly led discussions, respect for
one another, and openness to all moral questioning. Students themselves
should establish rules for discussion. Beyond asking students to justify the
points they make, instructors might ask students to consider who might
be harmed and by what. Students should be asked to imagine others'
situations and aspects of others' lives, whether it's others' religions, past
experiences, current relationships, sexualities, abuse they may have suf-
fered, fears, or personalities, and speak to what in a conversation might
disturb or be harmful.

In addition, the instructor might prompt students to decide how to
handle controversial topics and to consider whether information discussed
in class about people may be shared outside of class. What is unsafe when
we talk about sex and how can we make people feel safe? Will there be
confidentiality and *can* there be confidentiality? How do we respond to
people if they share something personal? How do we not force anyone to
share more than he or she is comfortable with sharing? How do we disagree
respectfully? And what will we do if someone violates the agreement or
gets hurt? What language might we use to be inclusive, to convey respect?
And is it possible to disagree while still respecting the other person?

How might a class decide? If a class suggests majority rule, I suggest
they read from Alexis de Tocqueville's *Democracy in America*, the section
called "The Tyranny of the Majority." Tocqueville writes that one of the
main problems in a democracy is that government can become slave to

the passions of the majority. Writing in the 19th century, he argued, "I do not say that there is a frequent use of tyranny in America at the present day; but I maintain that there is no sure barrier against it, and that the causes which mitigate the government there are to be found in the circumstances and the manners of the country more than in its laws" (de Tocqueville, 1899, p. 334).

Through use of this reading, the instructor can discuss with students why the class may not want to decide by majority rule and why individual harms may not be addressed if the class only abides by the majority. An instructor might offer consensus as a different model. The class might be asked to come up with a list of all kinds of words that are used to talk about sex and decide by consensus which words are acceptable and why in the classroom. If the class cannot come to a consensus, the students can decide to talk again during the next class period or they can institute a policy that when the word comes up, class stops for discussion of the word in its context.

MAKE IT INCLUSIVE

Acknowledging that some students do not identify as heterosexual is important at the beginning of any sex ed course, as well as is some discussion with regard to the language and differences between sex, sexuality, sexual orientation, and gender. The teacher should not be the only one responsible for inclusivity. The class can and should discuss ways in which they might fail and succeed in being inclusive. While SIECUS's guidelines for comprehensive sexuality education include discussion of the rights of all teens and suggest that sexual orientation and gender orientation be taught from age 5 through high school, Elia and Eliason believe that this can lead to a cookie-cutter approach (2010). They argue that this approach might essentialize sexual orientation and push for an assimilationist view that deep down we are all fundamentally the same. It leaves out a developmental view regarding sexual orientation as well as a view that identity can be fluid and that there are some queer youths today who do not want to be categorized as any one sexuality but for whom "bisexuality" does not work. They argue that the curriculum today needs more than simply inclusion, but also a focus that is anti-oppression, democratic, and that conveys a social justice perspective (Elia & Eliason, 2010)—in short, an ethics-based curriculum. In addition to focusing on oppression and social justice responses to it, it is important to acknowledge the strengths of LGBTQ youths as well as the important point that they too are teenagers, still developing, so as not to essentialize any teen as fully knowing, aware, and confirmed in identity, that is, as an adult.

TALK ABOUT TALKING

The language that students use in the classroom to talk about sex is an important point to discuss. Language can harm, and discussion of words like "slut" and "fag" and the harm they do, even discussion of hate speech laws and what they are grounded in, might be necessary. Many philosophers tell us how language helps to shape, structure, and provide meaning to our perceptions, our thoughts, and our experiences. Whorf describes language as "not merely a reproducing instrument for voicing ideas but rather is itself the shaper of ideas, the program and guide for the individual's mental activity . . . We cut nature up, organize it into concepts, and ascribe significances as we do, largely because we are parties to an agreement to organize it in this way—an agreement that holds throughout our speech community, and is codified in the patterns of our language" (1940, p. 231).

Sometimes it is uncomfortable to talk about sex in the classroom, so discussion is needed with regard to how students use language to increase or lessen the difficulty in conversations with sex. Why would they use different words with parents than with friends? What is the usefulness of slang, and are there patterns in the slang we use that privilege straight versus LGBTQ individuals? Men over women?

ARGUE FOR ADVANCED READINGS

At the foundation of a sexual ethics curriculum is the idea that students can think deeply about the ethics that underlie sexual decisions, attitudes, and behaviors. In this book I suggest a number of philosophers from ancient to modern in the field of ethics that come from a Western tradition. None of these readings, if given in parts, is too difficult for the high school student or that different from many history textbooks or readings they've already been assigned. When we dumb down the sex ed curriculum, we say something to students about what sex is, and this boils down to behaviors and rules about behaviors, but the philosophy presented in this book and in SECS-C (our ethics-based curriculum) invites students to examine sex in relation to other people and in relation to society. Advanced readings point them to arguments, justifications, and principles that they will use in the future to understand and orient their behavior and their opinions.

CONNECT RELIGION TO THE ETHICAL DISCUSSION OF SEX

A sexual ethics curriculum can't ignore religion. The Judeo-Christian tradition is at the foundation of many of the beliefs we have about sex today. If only with regard to history, what religion has to offer us with regard to sex is central to deep thinking about sex today. But religions offer more than just historical context. Religions provide followers with guidelines and rules for behavior that are grounded in philosophy, beliefs, and systematic thinking about what is good. Respecting what religion offers the individual student and sharing the precepts of different religions in the sex education classroom is more than just giving students a tasting platter of beliefs; it demonstrates a respect for religion in general and to a kind of thinking that integrates sexual attitudes and behavior into an entire system of beliefs and way of being in the world. This is what we hope for students in the future: that their attitudes, behaviors, decisions, and feelings will be integrated in an ethical way into their lives as they move forward in the world. Religion presents a way forward for some.

SUPPORT FREEDOM BUT NOT RELATIVISM

The problem with the FLSE curricula of the 1960s was that for some it seemed valueless—that students were given a lot of information and told to develop their own choices and values. Sex education was meant to free the student to choose his or her own morals. Students will indeed choose their own morals. But the act of "choosing" isn't just a matter of trying on various points of view. Instead, students must be taught in moral education how to reason ethically and what is an adequate justification for ethical behavior.

Through reading philosophy, by examining dilemmas of teens like and maybe unlike themselves, by thinking about the other person and what is good for society as a whole, by applying reasoning and compassion, students should then come to develop their views of what is right and wrong. But any view that states "it's all a matter of opinion" is not the view of ethical education. As Kohlberg (1981) once wrote, relativism is a step in the journey toward a more mature kind of reasoning about morality. And character education advocates do not include relativistic thinking as one of the virtues to which students must aspire. Instead, the virtues are traits such as compassion, fairness, courage, responsibility, humility, loyalty, and generosity.

Still, students will often question whether they have a right to judge others. Being "judgmental" is a fault, according to many a high school student. Those who say that people don't have a right to judge others mean three things: (1) *no one* has a right to judge another person because we haven't lived in that person's circumstances; (2) we don't have a right to judge another person because morality comes from culture and who are we to say which culture is right or wrong; every culture has different practices that are right for that culture; or (3) live and let live; don't interfere with other people's choices for themselves.

Curtler (2004), in his book *Ethical Argument: Critical Thinking in Ethics*, addresses these claims. He says that yes, we should always imagine what it is like to be in another person's shoes and which circumstances compelled that person to act the way he or she did. This is empathic reasoning and it is particularistic in that it looks at the particular situation in which a decision was made. But there is something unsatisfying about a morality in which every act can be explained or justified based on the particulars of the situation. As such there would be no universal rules. Morality certainly does come from culture and practices, and beliefs within cultures differ with regard to what is right and wrong. However, many theorists agree that there are some universals. For example, all cultures seem to have some rules about not harming others. They may disagree on what it is that harms another person, but they agree that there are cases in which when you harm another, you may be acting immorally. With regard to the third claim of students, that we might "live and let live," if we do so, we put ourselves in a situation of never taking a stand on others' unethical behavior. So, for example, if you see someone bullied at school, it would be important as a bystander to stand up against such bullying. To pick an example from the world of sex and sexuality, a recording artist may come out with a song that's particularly demeaning to gays or women or a minority group. It's up to the individual if he or she listens to this song and even buys the CD. Students might say, who are we to judge? But it also seems that it's a good idea to think through the notion that when we contribute to harm in small ways, we may be contributing to a larger ethic in society, and also to the injustice of who gets to make CDs and who gets to put their ideas out there and who may be hurt by those ideas.

Consider a fourth reason why students may not want to judge others in the classroom: they may not want others to feel bad. Sometimes students feel bad when someone disagrees with them, and if someone takes a risk to talk about certain experiences, it would harm them to be judged publicly for those acts. There aren't easy answers to this question, but a classroom that focuses on ethical principles and compassionate behavior can focus students not on the person, but on the moral vision for a good sexuality for individuals and for society.

CONCLUSION

This book is tied to a sexual ethics curriculum that I have been working on with colleagues and students for 5 years and that has been supported by the Association for Moral Education. Integrated in the text are thoughts and readings that are in the curriculum and available for teachers to use in part or as a whole. It is my hope that national initiatives for an ethics-based sex education will begin and that courses on sexual ethics will be taught in public high schools all over the United States. The current focus on individual health is important but diminishes sex and our responsibility to other people, reducing sex ed to how-to or how-not-to advice and skills training. In our now sex-saturated society, there is so much more to learn and to think about in terms of what is right and what is wrong than whether or not to "do it." New teachers can help sex education grow to encompass media education and education about consent, rape, and harassment, as well as about pleasure and love, among other topics that build ethical individuals. I hope that such an education can be the norm someday and that legislation that supports this kind of education is presented as a way to bring together battling liberals and conservatives, atheist and religious parents, and any group that has claimed a stake in sex education. But until that day, individuals, individual teachers, and individual schools will need to carry the torch and spread the word.

CHAPTER 5

Ethics for Individuals: Philosophy and Ethics in Sex Ed

In this chapter I advocate for discussions of love, lust, friendship, consent and coercion, and for the emotions shame, embarrassment, and pleasure to reclaim their place in sex education classrooms. While this chapter focuses on topics that raise ethical questions for the individual adolescent *vis-à-vis* potential partners, Chapter 6 examines topics that raise questions for the adolescent *vis-à-vis* society.

The ethical focus on sex education is meant to supplement rather than replace health components of curricula. Thus, this chapter describes how these topics can be incorporated into the sex ed curriculum and how philosophical readings can enhance learning within a sex ed classroom. High schoolers *can* read philosophy and use it to think through ethical issues. While other courses in high school require reading assignments and demand engagement with high-level readings, sex ed has typically implemented low-level workbooks and requests to simply think about ideas without using readings to prompt a deeper kind of response. I suggest, therefore, that educators challenge students in sex ed classes in the same way they do in other courses, by incorporating readings and discussions that are comparably rigorous. For sample exercises for the sexual ethics classroom see Appendix B. Each of the sections in this chapter includes an introduction explaining why the topic is important to a sexual ethics curriculum, followed by suggestions of what to include in its discussion.

An important place to start a unit on sex ed is with the feelings students have for others that move them toward sexual interaction. From a critical pedagogy perspective, one might examine the reasons that other curricula start with anatomy and hormones as well. Are hormones really what drive us as human beings to desire, to want physical and sexual contact? Some would say yes, but from the perspective of an individual about to engage in sexual activity, phenomenologically speaking, this student will begin with liking, loving, and/or lusting. And in spite of the light-hearted approach to sex that these topics suggest, there have been longstanding discussions in philosophy and religion with regard to them.

The ancient Greeks had ideas of friendship, love, and lust that raise questions for us today. Studying their philosophy also helps to distance the adolescent in the classroom from more simplistic discussions of who likes who and what was on TV last night. This is not to say that this is all that adolescents will talk about when left on their own. Adolescents are philosophical by developmental nature and philosophy brings into high relief the ethics at stake. In this chapter, I use both early Christian thinkers and a number of Greek philosophers as ethicists helpful to the sexual ethics curriculum.

The teachings of early Christians can be incorporated into a sex ed curriculum without breaching U.S. law's promise of the separation of church and state. St. Augustine (trans. 1955), for example, shared a tortured perspective of sexual desire as unholy using phrases such as the "slime of lust" and an itch that needed to be scratched by the senses. Augustine's questions for himself may not be so different from the questions adolescents ask themselves today in their most reflective moments. Students can read Augustine as a way to gain insight into their own feelings of shame and strangeness about sexual pleasure and feelings of lack of control. Although not the most sex-positive beginning to sexuality education, this kind of reading will encourage them to consider questions about the purpose of sex and the most moral way to involve oneself with sex.

FRIENDSHIP

It may not be self-evident why one needs to include discussions of friendship in sex education curricula, but a serious look at friendship can form the ethical foundation for discussions about sexual relationships. Also, today is a time in which it is common for friends to have sex (e.g. "friends with benefits"), as evidenced by some films, for example, *No Strings Attached* with Ashton Kutcher and Natalie Portman, and *Friends with Benefits* with Justin Timberlake and Mila Kunis. The message in these movies reconfirms what some might call a conservative view that one can't have sex with friends without romantic feelings arising. But they also twist the more popular view that it's the girl who wants the romance by having the boy fall in love first. Modern films and ancient philosophy can be bedfellows in a sexual ethics curriculum.

Aristotelian Philosophy

A discussion of Aristotle's virtues can be valuable at the beginning of a sex ed curriculum.[1] After studying some of his work, students can choose to employ an Aristotelian moral view when considering particular situations. Rather than applying hard-and-fast rules, high school students can be encouraged to make decisions by looking at the particularity of any situation, and improvising. Aristotle wrote that humans can become good at this strategy of making moral choices by cultivating a decision making process, developing good moral habits, thinking of our own temperament before making choices, having proper self-respect, and not letting feelings motivate actions and choices without first checking them with reason. All of these considerations can be part of ethical decision making with regard to sexual behavior and are wise guidelines for students. When I suggest that a curriculum start with the topic of friendship, I am also indicating that a discussion of Aristotelian ethics early in a curriculum can set the stage for moral discussion about important issues throughout the entire course. The discussion also sets the stage for a student's own justification of their moral choices.

Aristotle believed that the essence of what it means to be human is to be able to reason, and he wrote that through "practical wisdom," individuals can determine right from wrong (Aristotle, trans. 1958). Harvard law professor Michael Sandel (2009) writes that practical wisdom is not a science, but a practice of fine-tuning one's moral instrument so that it plays the virtues moderately well.

Virtues refer to the set of qualities that Greeks believed were associated with being a good human being. While Aristotle believed that human beings pursue happiness at every turn, he asserted that if they apply practical wisdom to this pursuit, they will choose to do things that bring to fruition their moral and intellectual virtues (Aristotle, trans. 1958). He wrote that *eudaimonia*, or "well-being," is the goal of life and *eudaimonia* is different than happiness; it is sometimes translated as "flourishing." According to Aristotle, when an individual is flourishing, he or she is activating the virtues. Discussion of virtue ethics at the beginning of a sex ed curriculum can stand in contrast to later discussions of ethics based on rights and principles.

According to Aristotle, any virtue of character must be enacted according to a theory of means. If cooperation is a virtue, then people should neither cooperate too little nor too much. If caring for others is a virtue, to be virtuous means to exercise that virtue in a moderate way. A person is immoderate if she cares so much that she neglects herself or cares so little so that she neglects others. With regard to sexual appetites, Aristotle argued that virtuous people allow some satisfaction of their appetites—not too much, and not too little. This idea of moderation is one that could be fruitful to a number of ethical issues in sex education and so it is beneficial to present it to students early in the curriculum. And this concern will not be new to students, many of whom struggle with whether or not they think "too much" about sex, or whether some of their behaviors are immoderate (Lamb, 2002; 2006).

Aristotle and Friendship

Aristotle argued that friendship was fundamental to the virtuous life because it helps people to realize their own capacities, and thereby promotes happiness. In his *Nicomachean Ethics* (trans. 1958), Aristotle discussed three kinds of friendship. The first is the friendship for utility or advantage. This is not the same as exploitation because many times this kind of friendship is mutual, but these friendships tend to last only as long as the two parties involved are of some benefit to each other. This may indeed be the underlying friendship in relationships called "friends with benefits" and can also be discussed in future lessons on consent and exploitation.

The second kind of friendship is a friendship for pleasure. In this friendship, individuals are friends simply because they have fun together. Pertaining to a sexual relationship, this kind of friendship would be one in which people get together for the pleasure of sex—no-strings-attached "hook-ups." Aristotle does not imply that there is anything wrong with either of these kinds of friendships, aside from believing that they generally change quickly and do not last very long.

There is a third kind of friendship that Aristotle recommends for people to live good lives and be their best selves called "complete friendship." These are also sometimes called "character" friendships or "perfect" friendships. In this kind of friendship, each friend sincerely wishes the other person well for his or her own sake. And in these friendships, individuals strive to be mutually known, to know the other and be known by the other in a very deep way. This concept seems a wonderful one for the sex ed classroom. To be known is both at the center of human longing and sometimes terrifying. What about sex speaks to this human desire and fear?

Like Aristotle, I wonder if friendship is the best sort of relationship, regardless of whether or not it involves sex. In the sex ed classroom, where some students have yet to have their first sexual relationship and others have had multiple sexual relationships, the topic of friendship reaches across the divide and presents students with the philosophical problems of dividing friendship from love and from lust and asking them what kind of person or friend they want to be to another person.

LOVE

Sex ed curricula need to address the relationship between sex and love without advocating that the best kind of sex involves love. While AOUM curricula have advocated that sex with love is not only safer but better (see Chapter 2), it is common for adolescents to do things for love that might not be in their own self-interest or well-reasoned. Curricula need to help adolescents examine the myths about love that they adopt, sometimes without even realizing how adopting such myths influences their behaviors. For example, adolescents hear about and may believe in the idea of a "Mr. Right" or a "perfect woman." They might think that boys are only interested in sex and not love, and that girls are only interested in love and not sex. Curricula need to examine the heterosexism in ideals of love that argue that males and females "complete" one another. When students engage with cultural ideologies they come to have perspective on their own views and can challenge beliefs that may be harmful to others if not themselves.

Plato's *Symposium* and Love

The philosophy I chose to teach about love is found in a story presented by Aristophanes in Plato's *Symposium* (trans. 1952). Plato lived in Athens and was Aristotle's teacher. One of his most famous and interesting pieces of writing was the *Symposium*, which tells the tale of a drinking party where a number of men share their views on love. (Symposia during Plato's time were held at people's houses and a large dinner was served, after which there would be entertainment or delivery of mock speeches.) One of the guests, a playwright named Aristophanes, sets out a theory of love that addresses feelings between a man and a woman, a man and a man, and a woman and a woman. (Such a discussion is surprisingly relevant to sex ed's need to be inclusive of all kinds of relationships.) In the same symposium, Pausanius discusses the dangers hidden in mere attraction, that is, attraction without love. He distinguishes between an animal lust kind of love where love comes from the pleasure associated with sex, and a more spiritual kind of love that is independent of sex. If a person gives in to animal lust, the person is a "vulgar lover," or a "lover of the body and not the soul," certainly a philosophy that some sexually active teens have considered.

Pausanius' view is closest to Plato's view, that the best kind of love is a love for transcendent goodness or beauty. It is possible to find that love in another person but if you do, it is because that person helps you to see or experience something above and beyond both of you. This view of love is at the root of "courtly love" in the Middle Ages in Western Europe, as well as the earliest Christian views about finding a transcendent love in God.

Courtly Love

I also recommend a short lesson on the concept of courtly love, an ideal that was prominent in the Middle Ages in Western Europe among the noble classes. Many of today's ideas regarding how to treat women derive from this concept. Courtly love wasn't a kind of love to be found in marriage, but a kind of love for a lady (as in lords and ladies, not just any woman) that put her on a pedestal. Modern students of sex ed can also come to understand that before this era in Western Europe, relationships between a husband and wife weren't expected to involve passion. Marriages were made to join families or for other practical reasons. It wasn't considered right for a husband to feel passionate about his wife or vice versa. Students can discuss whether there are some advantages to this view.

The idea of rules about the best way to love a lady is not only a topic that many of today's students would find interesting, but also one that informs them about just how deeply gender roles related to sex are rooted in our history. Today, there are numerous "rule" books about how to catch a man, as well as sex manuals. It could be argued that many have their foundation in Capellanus' *The Art of Courtly Love* (trans. 1990). Using information about courtly love in the sex ed classroom goes beyond a history lesson, however, and helps students today understand the divisions that our culture continues to make between pure and dirty, ladies and sluts, and how the word "slut" can be used to undermine the power of assertive and sexually desirous women.

In fact, discussion of the good girl versus the slut is pertinent to this unit, for courtly love did not allow intercourse, as it was believed that this would sully the relationship between admirer and admired. And "ladies" were differentiated from peasant women, who were not treated very well. Men were encouraged to flatter peasant women, bring them to a secret place, and then "embrace them by force" (Capellanus, trans. 1990, p. 150). In other words, men were given permission to rape the "wrong kind of girl," an idea that students should compare with popular and often offensive beliefs today about what kinds of rape are "more wrong" than others.

Courtly love was considered to be above physical love, as physical love was only deemed appropriate for lower-class women. Courtly love was conducted at a distance, involved a lot of physical longing, and supposedly yielded all the power to the woman whom the knight or courtier loved. The man proved the purity of his love through self-control. Men were permitted to embrace, kiss, and fondle their ladies—and they even could lie naked in bed together—but they were not permitted to stain this pure love with intercourse.

These ideas still hold some sway in their modern form: that intercourse stains a relationship; that sexual self-control makes a man more manly; that there are "good girls" who purify you. The purification of a man via good love can be seen in movies that pit good girls against bad or sexually promiscuous girls as potential partners for men, whereby the good girl becomes the moral motivator for the man's doing the right thing. Purity through abstinence can be seen in the AOUM curricula today as well as the purity balls and ring ceremonies around the country (Valenti, 2009). Moreover, coaches continue to tell male team members not to have sex before a big game, contributing to the belief that sex drains essential energy and strength from a man.

The quotes below, taken from current sex ed curricula as well as other sources, demonstrate that the idea of courtly love is still present in modern society:

- "Human sexuality includes deep emotional and psychological aspects and is not merely physical in nature" (*Positive Choice Curriculum*, § D2, para. 1).
- "Non-marital sex can undermine the capacity for healthy marriage, love and commitment; and that abstinence is beneficial in preparation for successful marriage and significantly increases the probability of a happy, healthy marriage" (*Positive Choice Curriculum*, § D1, para. 1).
- "When you 'hook up' for fun, physical intimacy begins to lose its depth, greatness, sacredness, and power to bond two people. Sex is shared as easily as a handshake, and the couple loses all reverence for the sacredness of each other's body. You begin thinking that physical pleasure is basically for fun and can solve the problem of boredom or loneliness" (Chastity.org, n.d.a, § 2).
- "Intense physical intimacy at the beginning of a relationship is a cover-up for the absence of love that failed to develop. The real love that you long for takes patience and purity. In fact, purity is the guardian of love" (Chastity.org, n.d.a, § 2).

- "This may come as a surprise to those who think that purity and prudery are synonymous, but purity has nothing to do with having a negative idea of sex. In fact, only the pure of heart are capable of seeing the depth and mystery of sex. For the person who is pure, sex is an unspeakably wonderful gift meant for your spouse alone. Therefore, the foundation of chastity is the dignity of every person and the greatness of sex" (Chastity.org, n.d.b,§ 8).
- "Abstinence for me is about romance. It has nothing to do with my relationship with God. It's definitely a bonus in that department, but it's nothing spiritual. It's about giving something special to that person you're going to spend the rest of your life with"—pop star Jessica Simpson (Young, 2002).

In these quotes it is obvious that the art of courtly love is still alive in various discourses in modern society, particularly in discourses about abstinence.

A discussion of courtly love may not only seem interesting to high school students, but can also lead into an ethics discussion about equal and unequal relationships, and whether such treatment is sexist or problematic.

Love as Illusion

There are other aspects of love that deserve consideration in the sex ed curriculum, for example the over-eager love of another or love as an illusion. Carol Cassell (1989) wrote about how women who feel dirty or ashamed of their sexual feelings sometimes develop an illusion that love is present in their relationship, when it really is not. She writes that at the first sign of sexual arousal, women tend to set up a love fantasy to accompany their physical feelings. Why do women do that? And why don't men? These are questions that are important to ask in a high school curriculum, especially when research shows that girls who believe in old-fashioned romance are less likely to use contraception (Tolman, 2002).

LUST

It's important to note that discussions about transcendent love do not always mention what exactly needs to be transcended: lust. St. Augustine (trans. 1955) treated this "involuntary" responsiveness as a defect in our beings, inherited as a punishment for having been kicked out of Eden. The philosopher Immanuel Kant (1780/1930) also thought that possessing sexual desire was demeaning to humans. These more negative views of lust can be set against views that are more sex-positive. What is important in the discussion of lust is to not reduce lust to the biology of arousal. Here, once again, our present culture has inherited several discourses that shape individuals' understanding of what lust is and what they are to do with it, discourses around the biological urgency of lust, that lust in men is uncontrollable, that lust interferes with reason, and that lust in girls is unladylike, which students can discuss given the critical perspective of the course.

Studies on Love and Arousal

How do people fall in lust? Psychological theories about the misattribution of emotion say that the "spark" an individual feels for another person might be a misinterpretation of biological cues. A person's heart races, he or she feels tense and excited, a little bit nervous, and hyper-alert to the other person, and the person thinks, "Wow, I must really be attracted to this boy/girl!" But is the person really attracted to the other person, or was it that caffeinated energy drink consumed 20 minutes ago (Hyman, 2010)?

One study looked at people's physiological reactions after they had been vigorously exercising on a stationary bike (Gollwitzer, Earle, & Stephan, 1982). With their heart rates up, they were then placed in a situation that would evoke some kind of emotion. They were in a high state of physiological arousal, for example, their heart rates were up, because of the biking, so when someone gave them a slight insult, they overreacted and became somewhat aggressive. This study reinforces the idea that being biologically stimulated, be it by caffeine or exercise or other factors, influences our emotional reactions.

Consider the study in which psychologists Dutton and Aron (1974) tested a theory of passionate love that was originally developed by social psychologist Elaine Hatfield. They hired an attractive young woman to meet some single men at the mid-point of a very shaky suspension bridge high above a rocky gorge, and to meet other single men on a much more solid bridge. The first bridge was 450 feet long and 250 feet high. The woman asked the men to tell her a story in response to a picture she showed them, telling them that she was conducting a study on creativity. She also gave them her phone number in case they wanted to get a copy of the results of the study. Only two of the men on the solid bridge called her, but nine men on the shaky bridge did. When some independent reviewers looked at the stories told by the men in response to the picture shown, the ones who were on the shaky bridge included more sexual images and references. Does this study say something about how passionate love is first evoked? Such studies raise interesting points of discussion for students considering the topic of lust.

Philosophical Perspectives of Lust: Greek and Roman

Consider the idea that lust and sexual desire get in the way of other qualities in a relationship. The philosopher Martha Nussbaum addressed Socrates' view of lust in Plato's *Phaedrus*. She writes, "The best lovers . . . deny themselves sexual intercourse. But this . . . is because they feel that in intercourse they risk forfeiting other valuable non-intellectual elements of their relationship: the feelings of tenderness, respect, and awe" (Nussbaum, 2001, p. 219).

These ideas about lust and sexual desire that were present in ancient Greek society were kept alive by early Christians, who took a harsh view to such very powerful feelings. Consider, also, one more ancient group, the Stoics, whose philosophy thrived from 301 to 263 BCE through the end of the Roman Empire and beyond. The Stoics believed that all passions were bad and that sexual pleasure was a particularly unsavory kind of passion because it interfered with reason. The Stoics thought, "Nothing is fouler than to love one's wife like an adulteress" (Noonan, 1986, as cited in Hawkes, 2004, p. 45). For this group, abstinence was the road to spiritual perfection.

Philosophical Perspectives of Lust: Early Christianity

If the Greek philosophers can aid sex education today, discussions about Christianity might also belong in the sex ed classroom. Insofar as Christian ideas form the basis of much of our thinking about sex in Western society, they will help students to understand the culture's and their own views about sex. Very few adolescents will make the connection between Christian thinking and their own thinking unless teachers address it directly. Most adolescents do not pause to consider where their beliefs come from.

It is important for students to understand that early Christians thought that the pleasure that comes with sex was not part of God's plan. In understanding the relationship of early Christian thought to sexual practice today, students can come to understand why a discussion of pleasure in school-based sex education curricula is taboo. In addition, just as courtly love set guidelines for dating scripts, so did early Christianity dictate rules about who is entitled to pleasure. This connection may be even clearer than the first. For example, a teenage girl can't look at a *Cosmo*-like magazine without being bombarded with messages about how to sexually please her man. While today there are magazines and the Internet, in the days of early Christianity, Paul's letters were influential.

Paul, the man whose writings form a good portion of the New Testament, was celibate and encouraged people to practice abstinence. When it became obvious to him that many people could not commit to abstinence, he asserted that marriage was an acceptable venue through which individuals could channel sexual desire. Paul also believed that pleasure within marriage was permissible because it helped people not to stray.

There are other early Christians to include who connect early Christianity to modern beliefs. St. Ambrose (340–397 CE) wrote that all sensations corrupt you because they distract you from the spiritual. In the 4th century, when Christianity began to become incorporated into the lives of many more people, it became clear that advocating celibacy was not going to help the spread of this religion. Christianity could not grow without procreation (consider the lives of the Shakers of New England in the 19th and 20th centuries, a Puritan group that died out because they did not permit intercourse). St. Augustine (trans. 1955), among others, had an answer that influenced Christianity and our own beliefs today.

In his writings, St. Augustine worried about his lust. Over time he clarified for all Christians the circumstances under which sex was acceptable. He saw the body as an "active battleground on which the war against lust was to be waged" (Hawkes, 2004, p. 58), and warned people to be ever wary of feelings of lust. Augustine (trans. 1955) was not just telling others what to do but struggling with these very issues himself:

> I came to Carthage, where a caldron of unholy loves was seething and bubbling around me. I was looking for something to love, and, empty of thou, my soul itched to be scratched by the senses. And so I took joy with the body of my lover, and so polluted the spring of friendship with the slime of lust. (Book 3, Ch. 1)

The church fathers following Augustine wrote rules about sex from 500 to 1000 CE, including: (1) sex should occur in marriage, (2) enjoying sex too much and having it a lot is wrong, and (3) having sex in different positions or in non-procreative ways is wrong (this was when what is now called the "missionary position" was first advocated, and it is named such because much later, when Christian missionaries went to tribal societies to convert the people, they taught them this position as the only moral position for sexual intercourse). All of these rules promoted heterosexual intercourse in marriage but they didn't promote pleasure. As Gail Hawkes (2004) notes, there were rules about when to have sex so that both people, but particularly the woman, would have the *least* amount of pleasure. The church fathers also discussed how sex for pleasure was harmful to one's health. Their rules also suggested some punishments for those who could not abide by them. In these writings, homosexual sex was acknowledged and considered wrong and punishable. So was masturbation, as well as wet dreams. Even in their sleep, people were held responsible for controlling their bodies.

Hawkes also describes sex in Arabic-speaking societies during the 7th to the 13th centuries CE (Hawkes, 2004), when there were writings of a different sort that did not treat lust as a sin. These writings were by medical doctors who emphasized the importance of sexual release for physical health. These authors taught that intercourse was a remedy for different diseases, and they believed that both male and female ejaculation was healthy. And perhaps most important to our current discussion, they saw orgasm and sex as a natural source of pleasure. There were other non-medical writings that discussed intercourse as an erotic art, putting emphasis on a woman's pleasure and outlining the phases of a woman's path to orgasm. When medieval European doctors found and considered these texts, they de-emphasized the ideas about sensuality, but did promote ejaculation as a means of health. Not all Muslim societies of the time were progressive, however; it is important to note that these kinds of beliefs co-existed with more repressive ones (Hawkes, 2004).

Lust as Exploitation

There is another tradition that deserves some focus in the sex ed curriculum also, one that focuses on lust as a vehicle for exploiting others. In short, this view is that those who lust after another person turn this person into an object for their own use, and in doing so, dehumanize this person and treat him or her with disrespect as they are making the person a means to an end (a way to achieve sexual satisfaction.) This tradition is exemplified in the philosophical writing of Kant (1780/1930). For Kant, lust violated a certain basic principle of morality. It wasn't about treating another person as one of God's holiest creatures, nor was it about elevating the soul to something that didn't have anything to do with the body or its needs and wants. Rather, Kant concluded that lusting after someone is a form of disrespect: "sexual love makes of the loved person an Object of appetite" (Kant, 1780/1930, p. 163).

From courtly love, to lust, to respect, these are issues relevant to the sexual lives of today's adolescents. Contextualizing these discussions historically can contribute depth and breadth to discussions that might otherwise devolve into a more shallow discussion of a *Sex and the City* episode or into "matters of opinion." I contend that it is always important for students to understand that matters of opinion are deeply embedded in our culture and have origins, the awareness of which can deepen understanding and help with future reasoning.

CONSENT AND COERCION

Consent and coercion are perhaps the most important ethics topics to incorporate into a sex ed class, and yet they are often neglected. One reason why this topic may have gotten short shrift is because it is a concern that is more important to the ethical treatment of girls than to the ethical treatment of boys. In popular discourse about boys and heterosexual sex, as well as with regard to the statistics of coerced sex, boys are the ones doing the coercing and the ones who need to gain consent.

How to gain consent has also been a bit of a conundrum. A popular YouTube video (Dubiecki & Reitman, 2004) shows two actors in the midst of lovemaking when one brings out a legal contract. Soon the lawyers appear at the bedside and negotiate the events of the evening. Once the contract is signed, the couple commences the evening's activities, certain of a mutual understanding. Indeed, the how-to of gaining consent in the middle of it all is tricky and so may lead a student to diminish its importance. Yet consent is the foundation of sex that is just, respectful, and caring, three important ethical goals of a sex ed curriculum.

Hypothetical Situations and Situations from Popular Culture

One strategy in philosophy is to play around with hypotheticals and substitutes in moral rules. For example, students might all agree that it is important for there to be consent from both parties for heterosexual intercourse. Is it important or as important for there to be consent for oral sex, for feeling a breast, for a kiss? The SECS-C shares stories about "stolen" kisses and asks students to consider the ethics of the nursery rhyme character Georgie Porgie Pudding and Pie who kissed the girls and made them cry, as well as 6-year-old Jonathan Prevette's story of being punished for sexual harassment when he kissed a girl in his 1st-grade class (Nossiter, 1996). Some would blame feminists for their vigilance regarding sexual harassment. And while sexual harassment is an important lesson to include in a sexual ethics curriculum, these stories of mistaken harassment serve to introduce situations in which the idea of consent is challenged. The curriculum takes the position that consent is important even in these ridiculous cases and that the primary reason stories like these seem ridiculous is because considering the offense and the age of the offender, the punishment is far too severe.

Another popular culture moment that would be proper fodder for a sex education class was the kiss at the 2008 Oscars snatched by a surprised and happy Adrien Brody from an equally surprised presenter Halle Berry. When he came up to the stage to accept his award, he grabbed her, leaned her back, and planted a big one on her lips in front of the audience. A conversation on the website Scarleteen (2003), a site that contains a wealth of information provided to teens from other teens who are readers, provides some comments about this incident, and they feature in the SECS-C as an example of teens discussing the morality of such a kiss and to introduce adolescents to this wonderful and informative space for information. Here are examples:

ScrltFan says: [2]

> I've tried to defend his actions to my partner over the past couple of days, but I just can't do it. I can't think of a reasonable defence [sic] for him. I'd say now that she isn't his property. My partner rightly pointed out to me that as a presenter in that situation, Berry might have expected that the winner would give her a peck on the cheek and maybe a hug, but that would be it. What do you think?

CR8ZYGRL replies:

> Ick, ick, ick. I saw that, too. And I am much less likely to dismiss it after he so rudely took up much more than his fair share of time, calling to the orchestra to stop, talking for at least two minutes. . . .
>   In short, no, it did NOT look to me like Halle Berry was okay with that kiss, and I do feel it would be appropriate for her to say something about it. Excitement and surprise doesn't really cut it with me as an excuse for that.

But CINNOBUN writes:

> I can honestly say I didn't see anything really wrong with it.

DREAMTEEN brings up another point:

> What he did was wrong. i am a survivour [sic] of sexual abuse and something like that would trigger me. 1 in 3 women are survivors. how would he know how she would feel about his actions. he violated her boundaries. (Scarleteen, 2003)

Thus, considering the kiss in a lesson on consent brings up a host of issues that are relevant to sexual behavior in a number of situations. These questions have to do with who needs to gain consent and under what circumstances, how some people prefer to be "swept off their feet," and whether it is fair to have different rules for different genders and different sexual orientations.

Explicit versus Implied Consent

There is an important debate today regarding whether explicit consent is necessary for a sex act, or whether implicit consent is good enough. Explicit means the person has done or said something that implies consent. This is an important issue to raise among high school students, who likely run into situations in which offering consent blurs the line between explicit and implicit. "Yes, yes, oh yes" sounds pretty much like explicit consent, doesn't it? And if a girl puts a person's hand on her breast, this explicitly says that it's okay to touch her there. But what if the girl puts the person's hand on her breast and says, "Feel my heartbeat"? At that point, someone might ask him or herself, "Is she flirting with me? Does she really want me to feel her breast? What am I supposed to do now?"

An example like this lends itself to further discussion from a different angle. Is putting a person's hand on her own breast morally right if the girl did so without consent in the first place? Is this invitation any different from a boy putting a person's hand on his penis? In the SECS-C, lessons switch around the parties, their gender, their sexuality, their circumstances in order to test principles as well as stereotypes. Is there an assumption here that boys need to ask consent but girls don't? That girls can be the initiators, and boys need to be invited?

Autonomy and Freedom

If one is serious about teaching ethics as part of a sex ed curriculum, it is important to distinguish between autonomy and freedom. Autonomy is something more than freedom. It is at the center of our respect for other people, particularly when we consider situations that might involve coercion or manipulation. Consent also brings up an important ethical concept worthy of consideration in a sex education classroom and one reviewed in the last chapter: autonomy. In Western culture, people treasure their freedom and believe in individual rights, especially the right to make one's own choices and to yield decision making to another only through a contract. Respecting someone else's autonomy must then mean respecting that he or she is in charge of him- or herself. And while others may want to persuade a person to do something, forcing them to do something shows disrespect for their autonomy. Philosopher Marilyn Friedman (2003) writes that to be autonomous, a person needs to be able to reflect on and evaluate his or her wants and desires. When you self-reflect on them, Friedman states, there is the potential for non-conformity and the possibility of rebellion against cultural expectations. Students learn about freedom ad nauseum in their U.S. history courses. In the sex ed classroom, discussions on autonomy and freedom are important to include.

Consider the following excerpt from the *Stanford Encyclopedia of Philosophy*:

> Generally, one can distinguish autonomy from freedom in that the latter concerns the ability to act, without external or internal constraints and also (on some conceptions) with sufficient resources and power to make one's desires effective (Berlin 1969, Crocker 1980, MacCallum 1967). Autonomy concerns the independence and authenticity of the desires (values, emotions, etc.) that move one to act in the first place. Some distinguish autonomy from freedom by insisting that freedom concerns particular acts while autonomy is a more global notion, referring to states of a person . . . . (Christman, 2009, § 1.1, para. 2)

There is more to autonomy than simply being free from coercion. One also needs to be free from others' influence, to make choices that are truly one's own and not based on, say, peer pressure. Thus, in the sex ed curriculum, a discussion of peer pressure can go beyond teaching kids not to be "dupes" to their peers and to be "independent." It can go to the very root of what it means to be an autonomous human being. Peer pressure is a form of coercion. In an ethics curriculum, students ought to learn to investigate consent for hidden forms of coercion, to answer questions regarding how much pressure constitutes persuasion versus coercion. An ultimatum like threatening to break up with someone if that person will not participate in whatever sex act the persuader is proposing takes away a little bit of the freedom the person has to make up his or her mind. It is coercive and seems to be more than pressure. This being said, a student in a sex ed class might argue that the person is still free to make up his or her own mind with full knowledge of the consequences. These are important positions to develop.

There are also boundaries to consent that must be discussed. Can anything be consented to? Many students in the sex ed classroom might argue that as long as two people agree to do something and they are of sound mind, they are on good ethical grounds. But what if one person asked another person to assist in a suicide? Would it be fine as long as both consented? The philosopher Onora O'Neill (1985) asks, for example, if surgery between two consenting adults is morally right even if neither had any training in surgery.

In matters regarding sex, how much sexual knowledge does an adolescent need to have to make consent valid? For example, a teacher can ask, if a teen believes that she can't get pregnant if she's on top during sex, does that make her consent to have sex invalid? If she knew the risks, she might not have consented to have sex at all. What about the developmentally disabled teen? Is his consent valid? Competence to consent is an incredibly important discussion for the sex ed classroom considering the use of drugs and alcohol among teens. The CDC reports that from 1991 through 2011 one-third to one-half of adolescents reported having had at least one alcoholic drink in the past 30 days; about 40% smoked marijuana, with cocaine and other drug use between 3 and 11% depending on the substance (Centers for Disease Control and Prevention, 2011). How competent must a teen be to consent?

Another important aspect of consent that is very relevant to the lives of teens is the concept of changing one's mind. Can a person change his or her mind in the middle of a sex act? This is an important question for discussion in an ethics-based classroom. Does the fact that it might be momentarily painful for a boy make it less right for a girl to change her mind? There are many reasons someone might change his or her mind, although whether or not a person has a reason at all may not make a difference when it comes to the other person responding ethically. Within the classroom, it may be important to ask teens what kind of behavior they believe is needed to show a change of mind. Is pulling one's body away enough of an indication? Is intercourse different from other sex acts with regards to the right a person has to change his or her mind?

Consent and Alcohol

What topic could be more relevant to sex education than this one? And yet it appears only briefly in most curricula, and writers tend to make a blanket statement that no real teen can use. For example, a curriculum might advocate that because alcohol impairs judgment, all consent under the influence is invalid. But how impaired does a person have to be to invalidate their ability to consent to sex? And what good will such a blanket all-or-nothing rule do an adolescent who is likely to be high at times when engaging in sex, similar to many adults?

In an ethics-based curriculum, adolescents should be given a variety of scenarios that trouble the idea of consent, imagining these scenarios between heterosexual, gay, and lesbian couples. What if a person can't tell if the other person is drunk? If a person asks another person to use a condom, does this mean he or she is sufficiently unimpaired to consent?

Philosopher Alan Wertheimer (2003) outlines several hypothetical scenarios regarding drinking and consent that a teacher can use in the classroom. He asks the difference between someone drinking a spiked punch unaware of the level of alcohol in it and someone who purposely drank the spiked punch to feel less inhibited and possibly hook up with someone. Can drunken consent ever be valid given that alcohol weakens the capacity to act on the basis of reason? Wertheimer makes the interesting point that if we, as a culture, really believed that alcohol totally takes away a person's mental capacity, then we would believe that all sorts of crimes done under the influence of alcohol should not really count. If a person can't consent under the influence, and he or she is not responsible for consenting, then the person pressuring surely can't also be responsible if he or she has been drinking, right?

Maybe not, but this kind of discussion is crucial in a sex ed classroom. In one study, when college students were asked to rate different scenarios as "rape" or "not rape," only 18% of participants considered the situation to be rape when the "woman was severely impaired by alcohol and/or drugs and did not have the ability to resist" (Kahn, Jackson, Kully, Badger, & Halvorsen, 2003, p. 239).

Consent and Age

The age of consent is a legal issue that can have serious consequences for young adults who get involved with teenagers.[3] The age difference between the younger person and the older person is an important criterion with regard to the legality of the sex. There have been drastic changes in the legal age of heterosexual consent to sex between 1885 and 1996 (Schaffner, 2005). For example, in 1885 at least half of U.S. states set the age of consent at 10! Today the age of consent varies from state to state, and is between 13 and 18. It is not only important for teens to know their state's laws, but to consider why these laws exist and what ethical considerations underlie them. The age of consent is generally applied to intercourse, but several states have established laws that deem groping through clothes, fondling, or oral sex to be illegal for persons under the age of consent. Some states have an exception for age of consent laws when the two partners are married or live together. At this time, 13 states have the "mistake of age" defense, which means that if an older sexual partner *believes* that the victim is over the age of consent, he or she might not be guilty of a crime. In some countries, the laws about age of consent vary by the gender of the person. For example, in Afghanistan, a male must be 18 and a female must be married in order to legally have sex. In Austria, a male's age of consent is 14 and a female's age of consent is 16. In the United States, gender plays an important role in that men are prosecuted much more than women for having sexual relations with someone under the age of consent. Thus a discussion of age and consent with high school students should also consider gender differences and reasons why these differences might exist.

SHAME AND EMBARRASSMENT

So far the topics covered address individual ethics. They are topics that ought to be covered in all sex education curricula in order to teach sexual ethics. Ethics does not only involve right and caring behavior but attitudes and emotions. It is important to recall that human motivation does not always operate that rationally. Feelings of shame may become connected to sexual behaviors and sexual feelings and thus to ethical choices.

Shame is an ugly emotion that can feel much worse than guilt (Tangney & Dearing, 2002). People feel ashamed when they believe they have fallen short of a standard set by a group one seeks to join or be in. The experience of shame is often one of feeling overexposed, as if someone one respects has seen the wrongdoing (Striblen, 2007). The root of the word "shame" comes from an older word meaning *to cover*; as such, covering oneself, literally or figuratively, is a natural expression of shame (Lewis, 1971). It is experienced as an inner critical voice that judges not only what we do, but who we are, as wrong or inferior.

While shame and guilt can seem interchangeable, researchers and psychologists argue that guilt is distinct from shame and connected to an act, whereas shame is connected to the self (Tangney & Dearing, 2002). When one feels guilt, one knows one has done wrong. When one feels shame, one feels demeaned, lowered.

An additional partner to shame—and perhaps even guilt at times—is embarrassment. This feeling seems to be fairly common in the lives of teens, but why? Like shame, embarrassment is connected to our sense of in-group identity. Like shame, it is built upon the rules, roles, and expectations that go along with membership in our particular groups. Shame can be experienced when individuals are alone; people can feel ashamed of themselves for thoughts, fantasies, or feelings that they experience when they are by themselves. Embarrassment, on the other hand, occurs in front of an audience. Embarrassing experiences are those that are socially unacceptable, whereas shameful experiences involve a combination of moral and social wrongdoing.

Lessons from Childhood Sexuality

Shame is said to begin in childhood, and so discussing childhood sexuality is an important component of a sexual ethics curriculum. Research shows that one-third to one-half of children play sexual games—and that might be an underestimation (Lamb, 2002; Lamb & Coakley, 1993). Some parents stop their children from doing this; some parents don't. What are the messages parents give their 3- to 5–year-olds about touching themselves? Typically they say, "Don't do that!" or "That's private! Do it alone in your room!" Some might even say, "Go right ahead! It's normal!" Older children play sexual games from "doctor" to "I'll show you mine if you show me yours." Children also imitate sexual content that they see in society. Some children will play house; some will play at being sexy dancers. Almost all of this play is done between peers and in private. Some adults say, "What's the harm?" Some say that this is wrong. How do we differentiate between normative sexual play and what could be harmful or wrong in children?

In an ethics-based curriculum, moral emotions ought to be included. It would be important to ask about the guilt associated with childhood sexual play and games, and also important for the sex ed teacher to understand that many high schoolers come to class with these secret experiences humming in the background and questions about normality hovering over their participation. A discussion around what makes someone feel shame about these experiences, and our attitudes about what is appropriate for children and what is appropriate for adults, could be a freeing and important one with regard to ethical considerations of boundaries.[4]

Parents, Media, and Other Influences

In a sex ed classroom in which one of the aims is to enable teens to both separate from their parents as well as connect to them, it is important to bring up the topic of embarrassment and most importantly, why it is embarrassing for parents and teens to talk about sex. An instructor might also ask about the pleasure people get from reading magazines in which pop stars have embarrassing or even shameful moments publicly. Why, for example, was it shameful for pop star Britney Spears to be photographed getting out of a car in such a way that it was clear she was not wearing panties? This made it to one website's top 5 "most shameful" celebrity moments of 2006.

Some of the times teens feel embarrassment, guilt, or shame are during experiences that may be important to their sexual health or sexual communication with others. Might teens feel embarrassed when buying a condom or asking a doctor about something on their body that might be an indication of an STI? If a parent were to walk in on a teen masturbating, would the feeling be embarrassment, guilt, or shame, and why? Admitting to being a virgin may be embarrassing to some. Watching pornography on the Internet might make another feel ashamed. If one goes "farther" than one anticipated because he or she got carried away in the moment or drank too much, might that produce feelings of shame? Guilt? Embarrassment?

In sex education classrooms, discussions about events that produce these feelings and others can center on the usefulness of shame or the problems that arise from feeling shame. These discussions might also include an identification of the important "others" one imagines looking down on oneself when one feels shame. Rather than taking the normalizing approach that comprehensive sex ed curricula tend to take, a sexual ethics curriculum could ask where the social proscriptions many societies have about touching oneself derive from. Such a discussion need not only address the history of problems certain members of society have had with masturbation, from the early Christians to the inventor of cornflakes (who also invented contraptions to keep boys and men from masturbating in bed at night), but also the ethics of masturbation. And rather than simply saying that masturbation is fine, not harmful, private, and so on, perhaps in a sexual ethics curriculum, using Aristotle's practical wisdom, and the ideal of setting up areas in one's life where one can get into the habit of good practices, is there anything about masturbation that might interfere with good sexual habits?

The Role of Fantasy

Fantasy plays a huge role in sexual development and sexual behavior and thus is relevant although difficult to discuss in a sex education classroom. It is unlikely that adolescents will reveal their most worrisome or erotic fantasies in front of others. However, teens do fantasize, and sometimes these fantasies are disturbing. Do rape fantasies cross the minds of teen girls or boys? Do pictures from TV shows such as *CSI* or *Law & Order* enter into the minds of teens with regard to sex and normativity? Do disturbing or not-so-disturbing pornographic pictures find their way into their thinking inside the moment of a sexual encounter? Research I am at present in the midst of collecting shows that for adolescents, it is not uncommon to picture pornography while having sex. While a person may have no real desire to act on disturbing fantasies, the idea of them can be just as distressing and lead a teen to ask if he or she is perverse, different, or even evil. A discussion of fantasies leads into a discussion of pleasures that appear to go outside of the norm. This includes the fact that pleasure is sometimes connected to shame, and that things we don't even find pleasurable sometimes infiltrate and occupy our minds. Unfortunately, discussion of sexual pleasure isn't always sex-positive. Yet all kinds of pleasures ought to be considered from an ethical perspective in the classroom.

PLEASURE AND OTHER EMOTIONS

If a sex ed curriculum takes moral emotion seriously, it needs to include serious discussion of other emotions besides shame. Jealousy, for example, is a "moral emotion" to the extent it can provoke people to act in ways that interfere with another's autonomy. Disgust is another "moral emotion"—what makes a person disgusted by one sex act versus another? What is it that pushes some people to pursue that which disgusts? Those interested in pursuing a form of sex ed that is ethics based will need to explore these kinds of feelings insofar as they influence our behavior toward others.

Pleasure is said to be an antidote to shame and one of the many motives for sexual activity. As noted in Chapter 2, the idea of teaching about sexual pleasure enthuses many liberal sex educators. Its absence in curricula has also been a topic for over 20 years, since Michelle Fine (1988) wrote "The Missing Discourse of Desire." In this article, Fine argued that sex education presents girls with a discourse that focuses on victimization rather than one that focuses on pleasure. Since then, many theorists and researchers have investigated this idea. With this in mind, what place is there for pleasure in a sexual ethics curriculum today? That is, what is the relationship between sexual pleasure and sexual ethics?

Biological Perspectives

When pleasure is presented in curricula today, my students and I have discovered that there are several prominent discourses (Lamb, Lustig, & Graling, in press). One is a discourse that is situated in biology and uses medical or scientific language with regard to what is pleasurable and why. For example, the CSE and EB curriculum *Positive Images* uses charts that indicate what is normal and discussions of the "excitation response" (rather than "getting excited"), both of which "medicalize" pleasure. Teaching about pleasure from this perspective "naturalizes" it and takes it out of the social realm. It makes it a problem or event to be dealt with by doctors and professionals in the medical field. In a sexual ethics curriculum, I advocate encouraging students to think about sex in relation to other people and not just their own bodies. Another is a discourse that indicates that knowing about pleasure leads to healthier choices. More negative discourses include discourses around pleasure and regret, pleasure leading adolescents into situations that will lead to STIs or pregnancy, and pleasure leading to uncontrollable sex.

Some have argued that teaching about *all kinds of pleasure* is a way to combat homophobia and teach beyond typical gender roles and sexual scripts. From this perspective, a sexual ethics curriculum that includes information about pleasure tries to move beyond a stereotypically male-oriented definition that focuses on genitals and sees orgasm as the only sign of pleasure. Today, Abstinence-Plus curricula, e.g. *Making Sense of Abstinence* (Taverner & Montfort, 2005), talk about the ways in which one's whole body can feel pleasure. While typical CSE curricula leave out some areas that are sources of pleasure, an ethics curriculum might introduce and name other areas of the body as a way to normalize this pleasure. For example, naming pleasure that is obtained through sex involving the anus can normalize it and combat shame for individuals who might believe that deriving pleasure in this way makes them abnormal. A sexual ethics curriculum also should acknowledge that pleasure crosses sexuality identities, and therefore that those students who are straight, bi, queer, or gay may experience the same kinds of pleasures. Finally, it suggests that what one feels at what place on one's body isn't the only—or even the most significant—contributor to sexual identity.

In this way, including the topic of pleasure in a curriculum could open up new ways for understanding sexual subjects. Louisa Allen (2007a, 2007b) and Moira Carmody (2005) write of an ethics of pleasure that moves us beyond heterosexual identities. While heterosexual pleasure is absent from the curriculum, it is detectable in some of the discourse. Teaching about pleasure in a way that includes all sexualities is a different way of teaching about LGBTQ issues than through discussions of tolerance, sexual harassment, or even the "it gets better" discourse. Why relegate minority sexualities to discussions of problems? This can support stereotypes, whereas the discussion of pleasures that cross sexual identity boundaries works against stigmatization.

Philosophical Perspectives on Pleasure

With regard to philosophy, an instructor of a sexual ethics curriculum might turn to the 18th-century Romantics, who held positive feelings about the forces of nature, and who viewed sexual desire as proof that the body was in harmony with nature. From their perspective, ignoring one's sensuality would be like ignoring one's humanity. Rousseau (1762, trans. 1979) wrote about the naturalness of sexual pleasure and sexual interest. He thought that society inhibited—and even corrupted—our imaginations and our capacity for pleasure. He asserted that society stunts our development, and teaches us to focus almost exclusively on intercourse with regard to sex education. Rousseau also argued that if young people are introduced to sex too early, their development will be harmed and they will not be able to use their imaginations to enhance their experiences. Moreover, the premature exposure to sex, because it is such a powerful physical feeling, encourages us to reduce all human relationships to being sexual in nature.

In today's curricula, pleasure is naturalized in the way the Romantics pictured it. But this very naturalness is also used as the basis of arguments that teach students that following that which brings pleasure gets one into trouble. The very pleasure of sex makes it, according to these curricula, hard to stop engaging in sexual activity once one starts. Because of this, many abstinence curricula say it is better not start. These curricula argue that the unstoppable nature of what is argued to be a natural pleasure can lead to dire consequences: STIs, pregnancy, regrettable sex, and even rape. In a sexual ethics curriculum, these consequences are important to discuss, but connecting these consequences to pleasure rather than to care of the self, self-control, care of the other person, and ethical behavior makes pleasure seem wrong. Remembering the Puritan roots of the United States, it may be that current attitudes toward pleasure reflect these religious beginnings.

Masturbation and Fantasy

If a sexual ethics curriculum is to take pleasure seriously, masturbation must be a topic. With its long history connected to shame and predicted problems, a sexual ethics curriculum can examine the ways masturbation might indeed harm a person without writing off this view completely as misguided and old-fashioned.

Today, liberals might argue that what occurs in one's own bedroom is one's own business, even when one is a teenager. But there is a strong tradition among liberal sex educators to advocate for freedom for adults with regard to pleasures and fantasies. They would be quick to argue that whatever someone fantasizes is ethically sound regardless of the fantasy, because the person hasn't acted on the fantasy. And if they are Freudian in their orientation, these educators might add that at some time or another most individuals have strange and even immoral fantasies, that human beings may even *need* to have these. If the mind is the most important sex organ, then isn't it imperative to consider what one thinks, believes, and imagines in regard to sex? In a sexual ethics curriculum, this question, and the question of whether or not one's thoughts and fantasies can be judged in terms of ethics, are grist for the discussion mill. In a sexual ethics curriculum, these answers have not been pre-decided by the instructor or curriculum authors, but rather are meant to be considered and debated by the students.

Women and Pleasure

Finally, another topic that some current curricula take up is the issue of female pleasure and what might interfere with it. Some theorists have argued that the culture perpetuates a myth that female pleasure is mysterious and difficult to draw out (Jackson & Scott, 1997). These scholars say that this belief goes hand in hand with a belief that the good male heterosexual partner is like a technician who knows how to bring about female sexual pleasure by being good at what he does. Thus, this set of beliefs makes sex focus on women's difficulties and men's prowess. On the other hand, philosopher Iris Marion Young (2005) writes that living in a society that sees women as objects makes women both protective of their bodies and inclined to look at their bodies from the outside in. Thus, if female pleasure is more complicated than male pleasure, it becomes so through society's views of female bodies. Some curricula give specific instructions with regard to what is pleasurable physically to a woman. But in a sexual ethics classroom, it is also important to think of all of those things that get in the way of female pleasure: a poor body image; focusing on how the woman looks to her partner; fear of talking about pleasure because it is unladylike to want sex; a desire to focus on a partner's pleasure rather than her own so as not to be selfish; possible abuse in her past; and/or having a partner who doesn't care about her pleasure.

CONCLUSION

In this chapter I have tried to show a variety of topics that belong in a sex ed curriculum if an instructor chooses to teach a course that focuses on how to think ethically about sexual behavior with regard to other people. While students need health information regarding pregnancy, STIs, and sexual self-care, this perspective is limited and ignores the ethical dimensions of sexual behavior and relationships. Indeed, *because* health-based curricula do not include discussion of students' values, this type of curriculum has made it more easily into many high schools. But students need more than accurate health information. If sex is a behavior that involves other people, then ethics applies. Students develop a way of thinking ethically about sex through discussion of love and lust, sex in friendship, how to give and obtain consent, shame, embarrassment, and the range of pleasures that sex offers to all people. And they can do so with the assistance of a wise instructor, current research, and centuries of philosophical thinking on these matters.

CHAPTER 6

Sexual Citizenship:
Ethics and Philosophy in Sex Ed

There has been a sexualization of modern society that has far surpassed what anyone would have anticipated 40 or 50 years ago. Sometimes it feels ludicrous to argue about what should and shouldn't be the content of sex ed curricula given students' easy access to pornography, websites with information that ranges from poor to excellent, television shows that vary from those like *Real Sex* on HBO—which today seem a kind of softcore porn—to those that have matronly female mavens giving sex advice like *Talk Sex with Sue*, how-to books, and sexual murder mysteries such as *Law and Order SVU* in numerous sources of media entertainment. Sexual scandals are a regular part of the news that students hear about high-profile figures, from presidents to sports stars. There is also a regular stream of images for teen girls with regard to what constitutes heterosexual sexiness, encouraging them to imitate porn stars and call it empowerment.

Sociologist David Evans (1993) first wrote about "sexual citizenship" with regard to who has sexual rights under capitalism and why. In his book *Sexual Citizenship: The Material Construction of Sexualities*, he reviewed the kinds of rights that children, bisexuals, transvestites, and those in other identity categories possess. Here I talk about citizenship as something much broader than the rights of individuals, although rights are indeed important and a part of this broader picture. In this chapter, I take the perspective of those who advocate for moral education as citizenship education. Citizenship education is a movement that asks that students learn, in public school, those practices that will make them responsible citizens when they are adults. Sexual citizenship requires students to understand international issues that pertain to sex. These aren't issues that make a difference to each individual personally, but rather those that make a difference in the world at large. This is similar to environmental education, for example, in which the goal is not simply to teach students to individually recycle their empty cans and bottles, but to understand what's at stake at a larger level with regard to the environment, to have opinions about environmental policy, and, one hopes, through voting and perhaps through activism, to try to make a difference in the world in this area. Being a citizen not only means being informed, but looking out for the community, state, and world with regard to that issue.

Evans (1993) writes that citizens today have become consumers, and that participation in society is primarily accomplished through shopping. He writes that an individual's basic human right is interpreted as the choice to buy what he or she wishes. He goes on to say that our sexual identities are deeply embedded in a discourse of what the consumer should obtain to express his or her identity. He tells us, "The material construction of sexualities within consumerism lies at the very heart of the modern era's instrumental self-interest" (Evans, 1993, p. 45). He also asserts that while sexual identity and expression are pursued in public, they are seen and felt within the private and personal domain. Evans, as well as theorists before him such as Foucault and Marx, makes the important point that external aspects of culture are often internalized. For the philosopher and social theorist Foucault (1990), the discourse about sex in society becomes internalized through our own self-management; it becomes the language about sex that we speak to ourselves. For Marx (1876/1992), it is a bit different. According to Marx, when we become alienated from the production of our "work," in this case, when sex is mass produced for consumers, we lose our spirit and authenticity with regard to sex. Foucault and Marx have quite different perspectives, but they don't need to be worked out here or in the classroom with students who are not necessarily ready to read Foucault or Marx or other classic works of sociology. Instead, students in a sexual ethics classroom are asked to consider:

- How does what's outside get inside?
- How does society or culture determine or produce the way we think about things? Determine our tastes? Get reproduced, supported, and confirmed in the things we say to ourselves?
- How does it contribute to or undermine a person's feelings?
- Are there authentic feelings that underlie society's discourses?
- And if there isn't an authentic feeling or thought underneath those that have become so embedded in who individuals are, what kinds of counter-discourses can be created?
- How can students and all individuals resist becoming simple dupes of the cultural moment?

If the goal of sex ed is to create future citizens who are reflective and deliberative with regard to society, sex ed needs to bring into the classroom those topics and practices that arguably interfere with people's rights or that may cause harm. For example, objectification, pornography, censorship, and prostitution are all social issues that deserve careful consideration. They may intersect with students' lives to varying extents, and they may never affect an individual student in his or her future, but as sexual citizens it is important for all students to develop attitudes, beliefs, and practices that are socially just.

These aren't necessarily easy topics on which to form an opinion. Those who are pro-pornography could argue for its existence from a perspective of individual freedom, or they might argue that some—but not all—pornography is harmful. They might argue that all types of artistic expression need to be protected no matter how minimally artistic. Students will confront these kinds of issues in general or personal ways. Personally, they may have to make decisions with regard to their own use or more generally, form opinions about the rights of others to use or make pornography. They may be victims, bystanders, users of pornography, or enablers of those who objectify women. But regardless of their standpoint, all students are deserving of education around the ethical issues inherent in making these decisions, and the practice of considering such ethical concerns as rights, caring, mutuality, and freedom will serve them well as citizens.

In the sections that follow, I include an introduction that explains why the topic is important to a sexual ethics curriculum, followed by suggestions of what to include in discussion.

MEDIA, POPULAR CULTURE, AND OBJECTIFICATION

The mass media has been called a "super peer" with regard to sex education for adolescents (Brown, Halpern, & L'Engle, 2005). In numerous studies, teens have admitted that their major source of information about sex is now the media, and in particular, the Internet (Allen, 2008). Yet few high schools require media literacy of their students and few curricula address it. While media literacy is not a panacea for all of society's ills (Gill, 2012), as a primary source of information, it deserves some scrutiny. At the very least, entertainment media's sexual scripts require analysis. And although advertisements are blatantly advertisements, there is one study that also shows that those students who think they are immune to advertising are most affected by ads (Greene, 1999, as cited in Gentile & Sesma, 2003). Thus, analysis of sex and sexuality in advertising might also be an appropriate topic for the sex ed classroom.

Why the sex ed classroom instead of a separate course on mass media and/or communications? Sexual content in media is increasing

(Donnerstein & Smith, 2001; Kaiser Family Foundation, 2007), and research suggests damaging effects (American Psychological Association, 2007; Brown et al., 2006; Collins Elliott, Berry, Kanouse, & Hunter, 2003; Huston, Wartella, & Donnerstein, 1998; Ward, 2002). The sexual ethics classroom is thus a place in which students can not only learn about the tricks of the trade that marketers and media producers use to "sell" their products—whether this product is a person, a behavior, or a thing—but can also learn what distortions are used. Misinformation about sex, stereotypes, myths, and typical sexual scripts can be analyzed to educate students as consumers.

Objectification

There already exist curricula that focus on teaching girls about media distortions of body image and the undoing of consumer culture on their construction of themselves as sexual beings. These curricula describe the narrow beauty ideal and use materials like Jean Kilbourne's videos *Killing Us Softly* (1979) and *Slim Hopes* (1995), which are standard fare for women's studies college courses.

Less has been done for boys, although advertising with regard to a sexy body, attracting women, and being virile has been aimed at boys at a fairly constant rate, from Axe deodorant ads to beer commercials (Brown, Lamb, & Tappan, 20009). As boys and men have power with regard to their gaze at women, heterosexual boys in sex ed classes also could benefit from media literacy instruction with regard to objectification and even heterosexism in advertising.

Philosophical inquiry would call for a consideration of the definition of objectification. What is it? The SECS-C defines objectification in the following way:

> To objectify someone usually means that a person is reduced down to an aspect or a function of their body. Most commonly, we talk about sexual objectification. A person's value comes only from his or her sex appeal or behavior, and ignores the whole person or their other characteristics. For example, a man is valued for his "six pack abs" or a woman is valued or reduced down to only "looking hot," regardless of the person she is or the other skills she possesses. (Lamb et al., 2012)

In this definition, both men and women can be objectified, but any sexual ethics curriculum needs to address that in U.S. society, women are more commonly objectified than men. The status quo argument might lead to blaming men and boys for their objectification of women, but it is also important to have a discussion about how the media present women to boys for objectification.

The SECS-C uses the writing of philosopher Sandra Lee Bartky (1990), who discusses how women need to constantly strive to fulfill a male ideal of feminine beauty. She is careful to write that individual boys may not buy into this ideal, but that there is an overarching perpetuation of it through society, media, and cultural discourse. Girls are asked to spend a small fortune on makeup, hair products, nail products, hair removal, and skin care products. Although boys are asked to live up to some standards of attractiveness and hygiene, Bartky argues that they are nowhere near as extensive as those for women. The ethical issue for youths has to do with the harm this may do to girls, boys, and to relationships between real people. While real people may be attracted to other real people because of their personalities, kindness, senses of humor, the way they walk, or multiple intangible factors, society sends messages that encourage us to reduce people to the way they look and to rate them on scales of "hotness."

Martha Nussbaum (1995) takes apart the concept of objectification in an essay of the same name. She makes the excellent comparison between slavery and objectification. She writes that a slave is no longer a person, but rather a tool for someone else to use to get a job done. Once a slave becomes a tool, the person who uses the slave stops thinking about the slave as a human being with feelings that are affected by his or her actions. Nussbaum also writes about circumstances in which objectification might be permissible. For example, in a loving relationship, might a partner focus on a person's body part without really reducing the person to merely an object? If it is pleasurable for both people in the relationship, could it then not be morally wrong?

While it may be interesting to discuss what kinds of objectification are acceptable, many forms of objectification and sexually demeaning representations are perhaps more prevalent and go unquestioned. Sex education curricula, save for the AOUM curriculum *Aspire*, don't talk about objectification, even though this has been shown to be quite damaging for girls in terms of their developing self-esteem, or, more negatively, depressive disorders and body image issues (APA, 2007). Curricula are currently being developed to help girls combat the images that are omnipresent in media with regard to the narrow beauty ideal or narrow versions of what it means to be a sexual being. While this kind of education is important, it might not make sense to divorce this education from sex education and to leave boys out of it. Boys are also influenced by sexual images of girls that are meant to attract them. Such images put them in powerful positions *vis-à-vis* girls' performances of sexuality (or at least place some boys in powerful positions). They are also influenced by media that requires a certain physique from them with regard to sexiness.

But learning to read media images with a critical eye is not necessarily the only or major step toward developing a stance outside of media's influence. Such an approach would limit discussions to focus on the individual. Instead, a sexual ethics curriculum wants students to think bigger and broader with regard to what kinds of art and entertainment are good and why certain kinds may be harmful.

Music and Lyrics

Certain kinds of music have been associated with objectification more than others and need to be brought into the classroom for discussion given that some students live and breathe some genres of music. Hip hop's roots are in African storytelling culture and rhythmic drumming; its U.S. roots come from the South Bronx, New York, in the early 1970s. Early hip hop was an expression of urban frustration with gangs, drugs, lack of employment, crime, few educational opportunities, and racism. The ethical position of early rap will be clear in any classroom presentation. However, contemporary rap, now considered a different genre that came out of hip hop, has a different feel. In contemporary rap women are used as background sexual objects to powerful rappers who show off their wealth and power. Scholar Bettina Love (SECS-C, 2012)[1] suggests, "The sexual imagery of hip hop videos and song lyrics exploits women, especially Black women, as they appear in demeaning roles throughout rap's 'booty videos' and songs" (SECS-C, 2012). Songs such as: "Donk" by Soulja Boy, "Lollipop" by Lil Wayne, "Bedrock" by Young Money, "Baby by Me" by 50 Cent featuring Ne-Yo, "Back to the Crib" by Juelz Santana featuring Chris Brown, and "My Chick Bad" by Ludacris featuring Nicki Minaj show male dominance and depict women of color as sexually aggressive objects for men's use. Comparisons of older hip hop to some of the songs in contemporary rap can help students examine sexism, exploitation, racism, and the intersection of these with capitalism.

Sexting and Privacy

Another ethical issue that belongs in a discussion of media is that of sexting. The discussion of sexting belongs in a larger ethical discussion of privacy and sexual citizenship rather than in a personal decision making discussion about what harm will befall a student if he or she texts something to the wrong person. Public Service Announcements suggest sexting can ruin lives, but the most recent data from the Crimes Against

Children Research Center at the University of New Hampshire found that only 2% of 11- to 17-year-olds sexted, and only 1% sent photos that violated child pornography laws (Mitchell, Finkelhor, Jones, & Wolak, 2011). The personal issues at stake have to do with shame, jealousy, and the respectful treatment of another person. The moral issues involve intimacy, sharing, and the risks a person takes when he or she shares him- or herself with someone else. But the social issues at stake have to do with privacy and artistic expression.

The SECS-C uses philosophy to explain these issues. In it, students are given several views regarding sexual privacy expressed by Fried (1970), that it is valuable and should be protected because intimacy depends on it (Fried, 1970). Philosopher Gerstein says individuals need privacy in order to have intimacy and argues that intimacy in relationships is part of what every human being wants (1978, as cited in DeCew, 2008). He says that intimacy without intrusion or observation is required for us to have experiences with spontaneity and without shame. Philosopher James Rachels (1975, as cited in DeCew, 2008) says that it's not just that people want to control information about themselves, but rather that maintaining our privacy gives us some control over our relationships with others. Anita Allen writes that in public and private, girls and women have less privacy than men (1988, as cited in DeCew, 2008). Sexual harassment, naming victims or accusers in the news, and laws about reproductive freedom are all ways that the issue of privacy is different for women.

James Rachels (1975) argues that privacy is important because "our bodies are ours and so we have the same rights with respect to them that we have with respect to our other possessions" (p. 331). This brings to mind several questions that can be explored in the classroom: Is a nude drawing different from a nude photo? Do individuals have the right not to have various parts of their bodies looked at? Do individuals have the right to expect others to keep intimate information about them to themselves? These discussions of our obligations to others and the protection of privacy also have the potential to extend to a number of other social issues that are important for students to consider. Moreover, they move students beyond only considering whether the passing on of sexting material is harmful.

GENDER AND SEXUAL STEREOTYPES

While bias and stereotyping are topics in social science courses within high schools, sexual stereotyping is more than likely not a focus of these discussions. But stereotyping and gender bias are crucial to an ethical discussion of how to treat others with respect and caring in sexual relationships and how to contribute to a better society by speaking out against biases. Stereotypes harm people, not only because they limit what people feel they may become but because they serve as a source of oppression. Stereotypes can be based on a number of things, including gender, race, ethnicity, and sexual orientation. As noted in Chapter 2, many sex education curricula can reinforce stereotypes of gender and sometimes race. Many also make sexual minorities invisible by conforming to a conservative belief that to teach about LGBTQ sex is to advocate for it (Henneman, 2005).

Defining and Understanding Stereotypes

The world of ethics in the field of philosophy offers writings on stereotypes. Philosopher and ethicist Lawrence Blum (2004) writes:

> A stereotype is a kind of generalization, linking a group to one or more general traits. By and large, the literature on stereotypes (both social psychological and cultural) agrees that the generalizations in question are false or misleading, and I think this view generally accords with the popular usage. It is false, or at least misleading to say, that Jews are cheap, Blacks lazy, Asians good at math, women emotional, and so on. The falseness of stereotypes is part of, and is a necessary condition of what is objectionable about stereotypes in general. (p. 256)

Blum (2004) also addresses the issue of whether stereotypes contain a kernel of truth, but he concludes that considering this possibility is just another way to apply the stereotype to an entire group simply because a few in a group hold an attribute.

While philosophy is important to an ethical curriculum, some studies from psychology can support an in-depth look at stereotypes. For example, some psychologists describe stereotypes to be cognitive shortcuts: They help allocate cognitive processing time efficiently and save mental effort, which is important since people have to deal with so much information in one day (Paul, 1998; von Hippel, Sekaquaptewa, & Vargas, 1995).[2] When people are under time constraints and are presented with a lot of information, they tend to stereotype more (von Hippel et al., 1995). With this in mind, it would be interesting to explore with students if they think this makes stereotyping more acceptable even though it is often inaccurate.

Blum (2004) argues that stereotypes are wrong to use because they are unjust and that when people rely on stereotypes they disregard a person's full humanity. He also maintains that false beliefs can lead people to harm others by providing a rationale for unkind acts. He further argues that seeing a group through a stereotype intensifies that group's otherness and creates a kind of "moral distance" from them. When people stereo-type other people, it is easier to do harm to them. Thus Blum begins with a statement about justice but appeals to an ethic of caring when describing stereotypes' harm.

Internalized Stereotypes

In the SECS-C, there is a unit that teaches about stereotype threats and internalized stereotypes. An internalized stereotype is one in which the person has assumed the culture's stereotype of him- or herself. Claude Steele (1997) examined the effect of internalized stereotypes by giving Black and White college students a test of verbal intelligence. She told only half of each group that it was an intelligence test, and the other half that it was not an intelligence test. The Black students who were told that it was an intelligence test performed worse on the test while White students performed the same in both conditions. The interpretation of these results was that a negative stereotype about one's group can cause self-doubt and contribute to a person living up (or down) to the stereo-type. This has been shown to be true for women and math tests. For Asian American women, when their ethnic identity is "primed" (made salient to them before a test) they do better on the math test. When their gender identity is primed, they do worse (Shih, Pittinsky, & Ambadi, 1999). Thus stereotypes act at an unconscious level and aren't always in our control.

The impact of stereotypes is evident in the LGBTQ community as well and this information can help those in the sex ed classroom to understand one another with compassion when stereotypes and harmful remarks emerge. Imagine what it is like for someone involved in campaigns for equal rights to discover that he or she sometimes has homophobic thoughts. Glenda Russell and Janis Bohan (1999) warn us that when living in a homophobic society, individuals all participate in homophobia to some extent and can't escape the stereotypes that emerge in their thinking or that might influence their behavior. One "cure" is to talk about these issues and bring them to light when they occur. Making the sex ed classroom safe is one goal.

Race, Gender, and Sex: A Historical Perspective

In the SECS-C, there is also an activity that asks students to discuss sexual stereotypes related to race and gender that have occurred throughout history while making clear that not all White or Black people were part of a homogeneous group.[3] For example, a poor rural White man's experience in the late 1800s was frequently quite different from a wealthy, urban White man's life. In the curriculum, there is history on lynching in the United States because it pertains to sex education, and the lesson points out that when the White community accused a Black man of raping a White woman, this accusation was typically made as a justification to torture or kill a Black man. The last known lynching in the United States was in 1955, when Emmett Till, a 14-year-old boy, was accused of whistling at a White woman.

This lesson also asks students to examine several cases from the late 19th and early 20th centuries that compare the treatment of a White man who was said to have raped a Black girl and a Black man who was said to have raped a White woman. In one case, the White man who purportedly raped a Black girl spent 6 months in prison, after which time he became a detective. Another White man who purportedly raped a Black girl was protected by the "militia" when it became known that an angry group of Black men were after him. The Black man accused of raping the White woman was brutally tortured and killed while the governor and state militia watched (Wells, 1997).

In this lesson on racial stereotypes and the history of lynching, it is important to teach students about the idea of "controlling images." These are images that those in power can use to control those who have less or little power. Such a discussion is also appropriate when teaching about objectification. The controlling image that supported Black men's lynching was an image of them as hypersexual, sexually deviant, sexually aggressive, uncontrollable, animalistic, primitive in their sexuality, and dangerous. In discussing this image in the classroom, an instructor might want to ask students how this stereotype is promoted and perpetuated today through the media and among peers.

Stereotypes of White women also played a part in lynching laws. Students can be asked to what extent these stereotypes exist today. White women were sexually stereotyped as innocent or pure, fragile and vulnerable, self-controlled, asexual, valuable, and the property of White men. Today this image often appears in the enormous media coverage of stories of missing White girls like Natalee Holloway.

Do stereotypes of Black women still exist? In the 19th century they were stereotyped as sexual animals, seductive, sexually valueless in the sense that their virginity was not valued by White society, and believed to enjoy sex with White men. Enslaved women were frequently raped by or coerced to have sex with slave-owners and male family members of slave owners. Black and mulatto (today, mixed-race) women, during and after slavery, were sometimes sold into prostitution or became concubines, providing long-term sexual services to White men for financial support. Scholars today have argued that these stereotypes continue to exist (Collins, 2004).

When considering historical material in the classroom, it is important to also explore the "norm" against which other social groups were measured. White men were understood to be owners and protectors of White women's sexuality. They were supposedly the caretakers of society, just, sexually civilized, and controlled. This stereotype helped to justify their lynching of Black men and hid White men's violence against White women, and especially against Black women and girls. Today, the stereotype of the White man as an upstanding citizen pervades stories of rape and sexual harassment in which girls' and women's stories are questioned.

Sexual stereotypes have played a big role in the enactment of harm to minority groups in our country's history. As such, consideration of these stereotypes today is crucial in a sexual ethics curriculum that aims to make responsible sexual citizens of high schools students.

PORNOGRAPHY

Teaching about porn? The phone is ringing in the principal's office already. But the issue of pornography introduces several ethical concepts that haven't been adequately considered in other lessons. A lesson on pornography could include an in-depth discussion of freedom as well as harm. A lesson on pornography should introduce talk of what's at stake with censorship and the problems and possible necessity of obscenity laws. Here are some initial questions for educators to pose to students:

- Is pornography harmful?
- To whom, in what circumstances, and why?
- What is to be done in society about those things that give pleasure to some but harm others?
- While insensitivity is not an ideal personality trait, is being insensitive a moral wrong?
- Is it an individual's responsibility to protect him- or herself from becoming inured to certain images?

Philosophical Perspectives: John Stuart Mill

The SECS-C introduces John Stuart Mill (1859, 1867) to discuss the philosophical and ethical issues underlying pornography. Mill's father was a follower of philosopher Jeremy Bentham, who argued that moral decisions should be made to "maximize utility"—that is, with the aim to cause the greatest good for the greatest number of people. Many high school students will have studied Mill already in their history courses.

Mill also argued that people should decide moral questions by looking at the consequences of an act. In using Mill to discuss pornography, students are thus introduced to consequentialist philosophy and may realize that many of them use consequentialist reasoning to come to moral decisions.

In teaching about Mill, students are reminded that while he wrote, "Actions are right in proportion as they tend to promote happiness; wrong as they tend to produce the reverse of happiness . . . " (1867, p. 7), he wasn't actually interested in the quantity of happiness but rather the quality of it. He believed that self-development was one of the most important goals of life and thought that people could understand happiness at a deeper level through educating themselves and going out to gain experiences. But he was clear that not all kinds of happiness are alike. He said that human beings could distinguish between lower and higher pleasures, and he wondered if it might be harder to get satisfaction out of the higher pleasures. His famous quote, however, is that "It is better to be a human being dissatisfied than a pig satisfied; better to be Socrates dissatisfied than a fool satisfied . . ." (Mill, 1867, p. 14). Students can be asked if it is fair to think of pornography as a lower pleasure that satisfies "pigs," and film as a higher pleasure. In such a discussion, a teacher can then ask students to consider what kinds of experiences are worthy of their time.

Free Speech Versus Censorship

Mill didn't believe that society should compel people to attend an opera rather than watch the *Real Housewives of Atlanta* on TV or search the Internet for porn. He respected the individual's freedom to pursue whatever pleasure he or she wanted to pursue. In this way, Mill brings into the curriculum discussions of freedom. Mill argued, in *On Liberty*, that people should have the freedom to do whatever they want as long as they are not hurting anyone else in doing so. He argued that it is wrong to compel anyone do something because it will make that person happier or because it is the right thing to do, or even because it would be prudent to do this or that. But it is possible to compel them to do some things if by inaction, for example, not getting an inoculation, they are putting others at risk. He argued that if a society protects an individual's freedom and respects it, it will support the person's own moral reasoning about ethical questions. He also believed that only by hearing a "collision of truths" will people ever come to know the real truth. Thus, from Mill's perspective, to invest in freedom in the classroom would mean investing in the presentation of many points of view, as long as this doesn't harm anyone. This phrase "collision of truths" can even be used in the classroom to welcome a variety of conflicting ideas.

Those who would censor or make pornography illegal argue that it harms people. Those who support pornography or support its existence in a free society often argue that it is harmless. Those who call it harmless believe that while it might be what Mill would consider a "lower pleasure," nobody should compel people to choose higher pleasures nor tell people what they should or shouldn't do in the privacy of their own bedrooms. Pornography, according to these people, is free speech and free speech can't be tampered with.

But students ought to know that we do restrict free speech in certain cases. For example, a person can't yell "Fire!" in a crowded movie theater if there isn't a fire, and they can't publicly slander someone. So if someone can prove that pornography harms, then the answer would simply be that access to it should be restricted, even banned.

Philosopher A. W. Eaton (2007) argues that pornography trains people to view girls and women as inferior to boys and men. Eaton writes that transforming inequality or representations of inequality into sources of sexual gratification makes it easier to accept, and even makes it enjoyable. It even makes inequality enjoyable to both men and women by enlisting our sexual desires in favor of sexism. Eaton maintains that pornography eroticizes the norms and myths of gender inequality and that by depicting women as deriving pleasure from inequality, from being objects of conquest to objects of degradation, porn is harmful.

Patricia Hill Collins (2000) makes the same case for the harm of pornography to Black women. She uses a quote from Alice Walker: "Where white women are depicted in pornography as 'objects,' black women are depicted as animals. Where white women are depicted as human bodies if not beings, black women are depicted as shit" (as cited in Collins, 2000, p. 170). Because White women are portrayed as cultural objects while Black women aren't, Black women are seen as less valuable and more exploitable.

Others argue that there is more harm in restricting free speech—harm to individuals and harm to democracy. The discussion of pornography as free speech is an important one to include in a sexual ethics curriculum. Former ACLU president Nadine Strossen perhaps presents one of the better arguments for students to consider. She argues that while certain images are offensive, the best way for a democracy to work with this is for citizens to protest rather than through censorship. She asks, "Have not feminists long known that censorship is a dangerous weapon which, if permitted, would inevitably be turned against them?" (Strossen, 2000, p. 7). She writes:

> Censorship, however, is never a simple matter. First, the offense must be described. And how does one define something so infinitely variable, so deeply personal, so uniquely individualized as the image, the word, and the fantasy that cause sexual arousal? (Strossen, 2000, p. 7)

She argues that the appropriate response to things that offend us in a free society is protest and argues that images of women in the media and elsewhere have indeed changed because of protest (Strossen, 2000). Instructors can ask students: Have they changed enough?

Catherine MacKinnon (1989) has an original argument that counters Strossen's. She argues for the censorship of pornography *on the grounds of free speech*. She argues, "It sells women to men as and for sex. It is a technologically sophisticated traffic in women" (MacKinnon, 1989, p. 195). More importantly, she says that the free speech of some "silences the speech of others in a way that is not simply a matter of competition for airtime" (p. 205).

There is another argument that students in a sex ed course might discuss, and that is whether *anything* "obscene" ought to be censored, restricted, or prohibited. An examination of U.S. obscenity laws is a good way to do this. Students can discuss who decides if something is obscene and consider items in the news like Janet Jackson's nipple reveal and the ensuing reactions during the 2004 Super Bowl halftime act, the obscenity trial of 2 Live Crew in 1990, or Howard Stern's 2004 forced move to satellite radio due to his use of obscenities.

PROSTITUTION

If parents are up in arms over pornography as a topic in a sex ed class, how might they feel about prostitution? The media that students watch depict seemingly countless scenarios in which prostitutes are murdered (see the *Law & Order* series and a discussion of it by Moorti, 2002). And while most students will not have had personal experience with prostitution, its representational presence in their lives can't be denied. Moreover, the underlying issues around prostitution with regard to individual freedom and choice, limits to freedom via the contexts in which prostitution typically occurs, typical relationships with pimps, histories of abuse, and entry into the profession at an early age are important aspects of prostitution to consider with regard to students becoming caring sexual citizens.

Ethical discussions about prostitution can bring in a wealth of material for consideration, from Marx's theory of alienated work, to Kant's theory of respect and the categorical imperative, to other philosophical readings on respect and mutuality.

Marx's Theory of Alienation in Work

Social theorist Karl Marx's theory of alienation is the philosophical aspect of prostitution that the SECS-C introduces. Arlie Hochschild (1983) describes this theory in *The Managed Heart*. She discusses an argument Marx submitted to the Children's Employment Commission in England in 1863 to make a case against child labor. Marx quoted the mother of a child laborer: "When he was seven years old I used to carry him [to work] on my back to and fro through the snow, and he used to work 16 hours a day . . . I have often knelt down to feed him, as he stood by the machine, for he could not leave it or stop" (Hochschild, 1983, p. 3). Marx was concerned with the human cost of becoming an "instrument of labor," and he believed that one of the costs was to the person as a human being, his ability to reach his potential, and his connectedness to his own self through his body.

Marx's concern with humans being used as machines was that human beings would then become *alienated* from their own desires and from other human beings. Arlie Hochschild (1983) compares the same boy to a flight attendant who, when she works, has to smile and love her job, and not just *pretend* to love her job. She argues that the cost of doing this kind of work is that a "worker can become estranged or alienated from an aspect of self—estranged from either her own body or the 'margins of the soul':—that is *used* to do the work" (Hochschild, 1983, p. 7). She uses the job of flight attendant to describe "emotional labor," and argues that most of us have jobs that require some handling of other people's feelings while women are more likely to be employed in this way. Hochschild writes that any functioning society uses some people to provide emotional service, which becomes a problem when people are exploited for this labor.

A sex ed class can apply this argument to prostitution and ask students to consider that most prostitutes do not experience sexual pleasure when performing sex, and many really dislike the men they are servicing (Farley, 2003). Is this then an example of alienation?

Kant's Categorical Imperative

The sexual ethics course instructor can also call on Kant with regard to his axiom called the categorical imperative: "Act in such a way that you treat humanity, whether in your own person or in the person of any other, always at the same time as an end and never merely as a means to an end" (Kant, 1785/1996, p. 36). This means that a person should never treat him- or herself as a means to some other end and shouldn't use other people as a means to an end. One must always also respect an individual's autonomy.

Thus, there are two of Kant's arguments that lead into questions about prostitution. If a person is to respect people as ends and not means, one would not support prostitution, but if what follows is a true belief in people as autonomous beings, then there would be no reason to interfere with their right to make autonomous choices, including the choice to prostitute themselves.

A teacher can ask students if they believe that one person paying another person for sex is an example of two autonomous beings making a contract and/or whether a prostitute, by willfully entering into this contract, is treating him- or herself as a means to an end, ignoring his or her own autonomy and capabilities. A teacher can also have the class discuss how different this kind of employment might be than other jobs that are exploitative, if it is at all different. In sweatshops, making sneakers is not in and of itself an act that steals one's humanity, but rather it is the way it is done, if it is done exploitatively, that makes it inhumane.

Some have argued that making prostitution legal would then free prostitutes from the risk of disease, physical abuse, and exploitation by customers and pimps. But there remains the issue of autonomy. To what extent are women or men who "choose" to be prostitutes *freely* choosing this profession? Martha Nussbaum (1999) asks this question about female prostitutes and takes a feminist perspective. She asks, in an ideal society, where all women were economically able to choose freely between jobs that would be fulfilling, how many might choose prostitution? Perhaps a few? She says that in this case, society should protect these women's autonomy to do so. But until that society exists, she asserts that the proper response to prostitution is not to punish prostitutes or make it illegal, but to find ways to give all women the freedom that comes with economic security.

Those students who argue that prostitution is a viable career choice might be asked to read philosopher S. E. Marshall (1999), who asks a few pointed questions. Should there be training programs for high school dropouts? Should it be a career option for women like cosmetology? And should there be licenses for prostitutes whereby they have to take a test, like cosmetologists, physical therapists, and others have to do, to show that they know how to have safe sex and how to perform their job in a satisfactory way? Should there be a complaint bureau so that if a customer doesn't feel satisfied by the service provided he or she can complain to a sort of a "better business bureau?" These questions sound ridiculous because it is difficult to regard sex as similar to any other product someone sells or a service someone provides—just like any other industry.

Marshall thus makes the case that sex is special and that it's different from other kinds of work. She writes that it is so central to our beings and our needs as human beings that it ought to be treated more carefully. Selling sexual services demeans sex and it demeans human beings. This is a crucial discussion to have in the sex ed classroom and is indeed a point made repeatedly in AOUM curricula. Carol Pateman (1988) argues that the prostitute doesn't just sell a service, as if this service could be separated from her or his body, but sells her or his body, and the United States has laws against people selling body parts. But maybe it isn't exactly her or his body that the prostitute is selling. It's not as if a john walks away with a piece of a person's body. Instead, what the prostitute sells is the powers of command over her or his body to be exercised by another. This has been compared to joining the army—making prostitution fundamentally a relationship of domination and subordination.

Gender Politics and Prostitution

Philosopher Debra Satz (1995) says that prostitution is wrong because it represents women as sexual servants of men. Supporting prostitution would be tantamount then to supporting abuse and domination. In this way, a woman's sexuality is viewed differently than a man's. There is evidence that for thousands of years, women who have been taken captive in military conquests have been rented out, used, or sold as sexual slaves. Throughout history, men have had an interest as a group in prostitution. According to this argument, men see access to prostitution as their entitlement, and their support of prostitution is an implicit support of this right. Real choice for prostitutes would come only after society was reconfigured to distribute rights equally, including the right to sell one's body and the right to use another's body.

In the sexual ethics classroom, we could point students to websites for national organizations that discuss these ethical issues, such as the Global Alliance Against the Traffic in Women, the Coalition Against Trafficking in Women—International, Standing Against Global Prostitution, or the Prostitutes' Education Network. These websites present data as well as arguments with regard to the exploitation of prostitutes and the lack of freedom/autonomy in the lives of many.

And perhaps closer to home, for many students the evaluation and critique of media stereotypes of prostitutes will be important. In the SECS-C, the movie *Pretty Woman* provides the basis of an exploration of the stereotype of the handsome, wealthy john lifting the prostitute out of poverty to be his wife. How are stereotypes about good girls and bad girls played out in this movie and in TV shows like *Law & Order* (Moorti, 2002) and *CSI*? How are the men who use prostitutes depicted? The movie *Born into Brothels*, which shows the lives of the children of prostitutes in India, might be another movie to bring into the classroom, as well as additional documentaries on the traffic of women. Global citizenship suggests that with regard to sex education, students ought to know about exploitation in its extremes.

SEXUAL VIOLENCE

Exploitation ought to be a focus of the sex education curriculum. It is both a health and an ethical issue, and its absence in most health curricula is cause for concern. AOUM curricula make girls and boys victims of each other's lust. But it is far more common that any victimization they experience will be in the form of sexual abuse and rape. Sexual exploitation is a continuing problem in the lives of children, teens, and young adults. Exploitation ranges from child sexual abuse to rape and acquaintance rape (Crosson-Tower, 2010). Child abuse and rape are morally wrong and our unit on consent makes clear that consent is needed in the practice of having sex with other people and that certain people can't give valid consent. But do students know why child abuse and rape are wrong?

Following the intuitionists' sense of why human beings do what they do in terms of ethics, it would make sense that there might be something in human nature that stops people from having sex with those who say no, resist, are too young, or even asleep. But it seems wrong to rely on intuition alone. Nor does it seem wise to rely on the snap judgment of a drunken college student, or a group of guys at a party. There is too much in society that says that exploitation is okay and understandable, and that it is natural to trust in people's intuitions to take care of others and consider them worthy of our respect. That's why the sexual ethics curriculum needs to address the *reasons* why rape and other forms of exploitation are wrong.

Currently, if sexual violence is included in curricula, it is typically part of prevention in which boys and girls are taught to identify consent, coercion, and caring relationships. Sexual abuse prevention happens in elementary school and little is done in high school to address the effects of such. Rape prevention is more often than not left to separate curricula (e.g., *Safe Dates*, Foshee & Langwick, 2010). What does it say about a curriculum when health is construed as not getting a disease and not getting pregnant, but not how to cope with past sexual abuse, how to prevent rape, or, more important, how not to commit rape? There is a feminist argument that I support which states that women should not be made responsible for preventing rape; they shouldn't be asked to avoid places or people or restrict their lives in any way because it is men's responsibility to prevent rape. But child sexual abuse and rape occur in contexts that support these acts, in part, through rape-friendly attitudes or through attitudes that blame girls and women for being sexually provocative. That is why a sexual ethics curriculum needs to address "rape culture."

Rape culture is a phrase used to describe a society in which rape and sexual abuse of girls are common and in which acts that might contribute to these go unchallenged. It indicates that there are attitudes, norms, and practices that excuse or even encourage sexual violence. In a "rape culture," women's and girls' bodies are seen as sexually available and men and boys feel entitled to access to them. This might mean that they have the right to cross boundaries that they shouldn't. This can have an impact on how seriously women are taken when they say no, on the ability to say no, and how entitled a girl feels to avoid or disclose sexual abuse.

Rape myths, as well as myths about child sexual abuse, can be presented to high school students studying sexual ethics, and these myths are readily available online (including a few in Appendix C). They express myths regarding who gets raped, if women lie about rape, if women ask for it, and if children can fully participate in sex with someone older and/or more powerful than they are.

Having a stance on whether a rape occurred or not is a moral act or judgment. French politician Dominique Strauss-Kahn was accused of an attempted rape of a hotel maid in 2011. Media coverage indicated many connected to the politician attempted to prove that the chamber maid was lying or set up by political opponents. The fact that she had lied on an immigration document was used to suggest that she would then lie about a rape and that this was another he said/she said story. The idea of "gray rape" was discussed in the popular press when, in 2011, Whoopi Goldberg called a rape not "rape rape" on national TV when speaking of an acquaintance rape. She was referring to film director Roman Polanski, who had been charged with the sexual assault of a 13-year-old female. At a party, after giving her alcohol and pills, he had sex with her (raped her) in a hot tub. By claiming that this incident was not an example of "rape rape" Goldberg perpetuated a myth that "real rape" only occurs when strangers jump out of bushes on dark nights and force sexually innocent women to have sex at gunpoint. In this scenario, the rapist is usually pictured as ugly and brutish, and the victim is young, "pure," pretty and White.

This problem of referring to some rapes as "legitimate" and others as not made the news in 2012 when a U.S. congressman, Todd Akin, said publicly that women can't get pregnant from rape: "From what I understand from doctors . . . if it's a legitimate rape, the female body has ways to try to shut that whole thing down" (quoted in Badash, 2012, para. 2). Widespread media attention to this remark almost forced the Missouri congressman to step down from his seat. He eventually lost his bid for reelection.

Research by Kahn et al. (2003) has shown that college students too are confused about what is and isn't rape. When female students were asked if anyone had ever forced them to have sex, 57% of those who said yes did not call it rape. If they had been drinking, they did not call it rape.

If they knew the man, they were less likely to call it rape. If they hadn't fought him, if there were no weapons, or if he bought dinner, then they were less likely to call it rape.

Rape culture doesn't only excuse rape, but makes it hard for victims to be believed and to get the empathy as well as the services they deserve. Research shows victims are harmed by the negative reactions they receive, and some have even called this a second victimization.

What philosophy is brought to bear on this topic? Readings on autonomy and freedom are still as pertinent as they were in discussions of consent. In an ethics-based sex education course, the important philosophical questions are whether sex is a special category and sexual harm greater than other harms, who has the ability to consent, and whether a violation of one's right to consent to sex or an uncaring and even brutal act that is sexual is worse than other acts.

RELIGION

The separation of church and state, one of the founding principles of our democracy, might suggest that religion has no place in a sex education classroom. But this would be wrong. Progressives have long associated sex education with secularism (Rasmussen, 2010), seeing religion as a "regressive force in the world, one that in its dogmatism is not amenable to change, dialogue, or non-violent resolutions" (Jakobsen & Pellegrini, 2008, p. 2). Teaching students what stances different religions take with regard to sex, and that religion offers some answers, is not only appropriate but crucial for sexual citizenship. Most religions do not set down arbitrary rules about sexual practice to be followed without question. Instead, religions often give arguments, reasons, and even leeway with regard to what is right and wrong. Religious teachings discuss when, how, and with whom it is ethical to engage in sex. They also contain writings about homosexuality, birth control, masturbation, pleasure, and more. Most religions have wide variations with regard to how permissive or restrictive they are; that is, they have more liberal and more conservative variations, and people who are followers of most religions argue amongst themselves with regard to the interpretation of texts and rules. Religions also change over time, leading to additional versions and variations in practices. What is advised in a primary text, like the Bible, may no longer be what is advised by parents or by ministers. Teachers will want students to understand the variability within each religion as well as to think about how their own religion and the religions of others have responded to changes in modern society.

Including religion may also be a way to address some of the problems conservatives in the United States have with sex education as it currently exists. Conservatives have argued that sex ed that is aimed at teaching only the "how-tos" of sex and prevention with no values attached actually imparts a value to students—the value that whatever they *feel* is right, *is* right.

Many students don't actually know the teachings of their own religion about sex and sexuality even if they are regular attendees at their place of worship. Sex educators who ignore how deeply entangled religious and non-religious communities are in the United States and elsewhere do a disservice to students. Knowing the diversity in religious perspectives can help a student deepen his or her understanding of his or her own religious background, as well as appreciate that there are differences in the world that guide different expressions and practices. Thus teaching about various religions' attitudes and practices about sex can honor individual students' histories and families, can contribute to respect for others' beliefs, and can help students understand the ethical grounding of what might seem to them to be arbitrary rules that come down "from above."

Western and Eastern Perspectives

Including religious teachings is akin to including philosophy. An overview of Western and Eastern religions is a good place to start. Rather than focusing on the restrictions that religions put on sexual behavior, it is important to begin with more affirming lessons. For example, Hinduism is very affirming of sex and sexuality. The four goals of Hindu devotion include *Dharma* (virtue), *Artha* (financial well-being), *Moksha* (spiritual liberation), and *Kama* (pleasure). *Parapremarupa* (ultimate love) leads to "perfection, immortality, and fulfillment" (Howell, 2007). Buddhism views sexuality as part of humans' desires, fears, needs, and intentions, and teaches that liberation manifests itself in ever-increasing compassion for others. People must transcend their desire for that which is harmful or transient, for those longings will lead to suffering and dissatisfaction. In Shintoism, sexual energy is celebrated as spiritual energy that comes from fertility. The Navajo saw sex as a blessing from the spiritual world. In both Western and Eastern religions, there are beautiful poetic and cultural expressions of human sexuality amidst regulations and admonitions that sexual love should take place in the context of a monogamous, heterosexual union. Students in the sexual ethics classroom can consider the importance of monogamy to religion as well as explore those places that either emphasize or deemphasize heterosexuality.

Transcendence

The teacher might also take special note of the emphasis on transcendence in many religions and the separation of body and spirit. Students can be asked to consider the phrase "your body is a temple" to explore the meaning of virginity, and to think about why virginity is seen as more important for a woman than a man. Restraint is also connected to transcendence, purity, and abstinence. Some religions ask devout followers to fast or give up bodily pleasures such as food. Some ask certain members to maintain celibacy. Is the "ecstasy" that some religions talk about, the overwhelming feeling of peace and oneness with God, related to sexuality in some way? Is it a substitute of or representation of it? Instructors can ask students to consider why it is that most religions take sex very seriously.

In an ethics-based sex education curriculum students can study the Koran and Sharia law, the Bhagavad Gita, the Kama Sutra, the Bible, the Torah, and more. Instructors can ask students to study their own or another's religion by talking to a leader in their place of worship, talking to their parents, or doing library research. Giving students the tools to ask about sexual guidance as a function of religion will also help them to research those questions that fall outside of religion. And the ethics-based sex ed teacher who can bring religious leaders from the community into the classroom to discuss their religions' points of view regarding sex shows respect for religions' views and teaches such respect to the students as well.

SEXUAL RIGHTS

An ethical consideration of sex wouldn't be complete without a look at the laws formed around who can have sex with whom and the justification of such laws. Marriage laws and challenges to them stem from an ethical view about the sexual nature of the marriage relationship. In a sexual ethics curriculum, students ought to consider the changing nature of these laws, their history, and the right of the state or federal government to decide what constitutes an appropriate sexual partner and an appropriate sexual act.

Legal Issues

Laws about sexuality have a long history, and these laws have been fought one by one by advocates of gay and lesbian rights. Some of the first legal battles concern sodomy laws. Sodomy, defined as oral and/or anal sex, was illegal since colonial times, when this "crime against nature" could receive a death sentence. These acts were classified as felonies until 2003.

Legally, much is up in the air. Many states have passed laws that prohibit discrimination in employment, housing, or other services. Laws against LGBTQ individuals serving openly in the military, known as "Don't Ask, Don't Tell," were repealed in 2011. Marriage between two people of the same gender is possible in six states and eleven countries (as of 2012).

The question for the sexual ethics classroom is if there is any justifiable reason to not give the same rights to individuals based on whom they have sex with. In this discussion, religiously based arguments may arise, as well as arguments that define family and marriage in such a way as to prevent or procure those rights. The idea of sex for procreation as "natural" will be called into question in terms of what is indeed "natural," given the presence and number of LGBTQ individuals in most cultures and the large amount of non-procreational sex that is currently acceptable in our culture. Also, the idea that many families are formed without reproductive sex between the two parents (e.g., through adoption, surrogacy, or artificial insemination) calls into question the idea that there can be only one way to form a family.

Philosophy and Human Rights

There are so many philosophers in the Western tradition who speak to justice and rights that the instructor will have any number to choose from. Indeed, Rawls's (1971) "veil of ignorance" strategy for determining the laws of a society might be an interesting reading with regard to fairness. The students would be asked, if one were to be plopped down into this society with a set of very particular attributes, attachments, preferences, and desires, what laws would be fair to both one's self and to others?

Another philosophical piece that was circulated when the fight for same-sex marriage began came from feminist philosopher Claudia Card (1996), who argued that the institution of marriage is so problematic and tied to so many unethical acts that it wasn't worthy of this struggle. She writes that currently male heads of households get away with battering, incest, and even murder, which suggests that the "family" is not an institution to be imitated (Card, 1996).

The rights of LGBTQ individuals are in such flux that it is difficult to set them to paper lest they change in the year before publication. However, these laws are intimately connected to societal attitudes and feelings about sexual relations between same-sex individuals. As with all topics in the sexual ethics curriculum, students should be invited to come to their own opinions, if they can justify them ethically. Religion may be a source of justification for some. But from the perspective of justice or caring, it will be hard for students to argue against the rights of other citizens.

CONCLUSION

In this chapter I have tried to show a variety of topics that belong in a sex ed curriculum in order to take seriously the charge that education needs to create citizens for a new world. This new world is one in which sex is everywhere and ethical dilemmas surrounding sex are presented at every turn. It's a world in which religion still plays a major role in setting out guidelines for sexual behavior with rational as well as spiritual reasons for abiding by these guidelines. It is a world where exploitation and sexual harm continue to take place, and in which we are asked to numb ourselves to this violence and not question the harm done to those who are most in need of care. In short, if sex is one aspect of our lives that makes us deeply human, then how we respond to the sex around us is a deeply ethical question. This is indeed one of the primary reasons for any education to create thoughtful and responsive citizens in all matters and with particular attention to relationships.

Discussion Questions and Activities for Future Educators

with Kaelin Farmer

Chapter 1

1. In addition to providing information about health care to students and teaching adolescents ways in which they can become good sexual citizens, what other benefits can sex education offer to students?
2. Do sexuality educators have a moral obligation to address topics such as sexual violence, homophobia, pornography, and the ethics of sexual behavior? Does sex positivity have a place in sex education? In schools?
3. To what degree should students' questions about sexual health and sexuality as well as their own developing beliefs, opinions, and moral arguments guide the direction, content, or tenor of a sex ed course? Pick a city to use as an example: Do the current legal requirements of this local area and of its state allow for the degree of democratic education you feel is ideal? What about on a federal level? Would such a program be able to get funding?
4. Go to a bookstore or library and find a book about sex ed geared toward younger kids and preteens. Deconstruct this book from your own point of view. How much information is given? Is the book too detailed or not detailed enough? What are some of the issues involving sex ed for younger kids? Analyze the language in the book; for example, does the book use the word "vulva" instead of "vagina"? Why?

Example books:

- Bailey, J., & McCafferty, J. (2004). *Sex, puberty, and all that stuff: A guide to growing up*. Hauppauge, NY: Barron's Educational Series.

- Brown, L. K., & Brown, M. (2000). *What's the big secret?: Talking about sex with girls and boys.* Boston: Little, Brown and Company.
- Cole, J., & Tiegreen, A. (2009). *Asking about sex and growing up: A question-and-answer book for boys and girls.* New York: HarperCollins.
- Gitchel, S., & Foster L. (2005). *Let's talk about S-E-X: A guide for kids 9 to 12 and their parents.* Excelsior, MN: The Book Peddlers.
- Harris, R. H., & Emberley, M. (2009). *It's perfectly normal: Changing bodies, growing up, sex, and sexual health (the family library).* Somerville, MA: Candlewick Press.
- Saltz, G., & Cravath, L. A. (2008). *Amazing you!: Getting smart about your private parts.* New York: Puffin Books.

5. Take a look at one of the sexuality forums for teens listed in Appendix D. What sort of questions are teens asking? What topics are they discussing? Do you believe the questions and topics you have seen being discussed by teens can or should be addressed in sex ed? Why or why not?
6. Pick one of the pieces of sex ed–related legislation that has come out since 1990, such as the Eight Tenets of Abstinence (1996), the Children and Families Community-Based Abstinence-Education (CBAE) Program (2001), or the Repealing Ineffective and Incomplete Abstinence-Only Program Funding Act (2011). How have they impacted the prevalence of AOUM education in the late 20th and early 21st centuries? Abstinence-based sex education is usually seen as a conservative preference, but practically speaking both Republican and Democrat administrations have supported AOUM. Why do you think this is? Consider documents such as the Kirby analyses (2001, 2002, 2007), the Waxman Report (2004), or Trenholm et al.'s (2007) report in Mathematica Policy Research.

Chapter 2

1. How is the sex ed that you received as a child or an adolescent different from currently available sex education? What trends and changes in mainstream sex education offered to children and adolescents have you observed in your lifetime? If these trends continue into the future, what positive or negative consequences do you anticipate?
2. Consider the idea that withholding knowledge works against a person developing independence. Can you think of other ways (not mentioned in this chapter) in which withholding fully comprehensive sex ed from young people limits their agency?

Remember that teenagers do not exist in a void—many will have access to other sources of information about sexuality, be this their parents or friends, the Internet, pornography, television, film, or popular music. Does sex ed hold a unique position and responsibility among these sources of information, or might we just let teens search for information themselves?

3. One criticism of sex education that teaches more than abstinence is that it suggests that students ought to be having sex. What are the messages that are being sent to teens today about who they are sexually? If we tell teens that they are immature, irresponsible, and in denial regarding the consequences of sex, what outcomes should we expect? What messages could result in a more positive outcome? Give two or three examples.

4. What roles have the presence, absence, or distortion of scientific evidence played in the evolution of sex ed?

5. Using any source you like (Internet search, news articles, pop culture), can you find an example of inaccurate information about sexuality directed toward teenagers? Discuss why this particular example is problematic. (Hint: check the SIECUS and Advocates for Youth websites).

6. How does a sex ed curriculum that ignores or demonizes queerness and/or LGBTQ identities fail *all* its students, gay and straight alike? Feel free to draw on outside sources, or refer to Appendix D.

7. White middle-class bias in sex ed is not the sole providence of either conservative or liberal attitudes, and can be seen in CSE as well as AOUM education. What changes would be needed in curricula to address this?

8. Do you believe it is important to teach adolescents that sex can and should be pleasurable? Why or why not? A *New York Times* article, "Teaching Good Sex" (Abraham, 2011), gives an example of sex ed that does encompass pleasure. What are your thoughts on this curriculum?

9. An op-ed in the *New York Times* asked, "Does Sex Ed Undermine Parental Rights?" (George & Moschella, 2011). Are adults' rights to religious freedom the same as their rights to parent their children as they see fit? Should parents have the right to withdraw their child from sex ed? How would you justify sex ed being mandatory for all children, no matter what? At what age and why should it be mandatory then and not earlier?

10. Choose an example of gender stereotypes in sex education. Discuss in more depth what is problematic about this example of gender stereotypes, and what messages it sends to adolescents.

Chapter 3

1. Do you agree that there are some values that are universally desirable in a good citizen such as respect for self and others, responsibility, self-discipline, self-control, integrity, honesty, fairness, and kindness? Are these the same values we should apply to "sexual citizens"? What do you think of the phrase "sexual citizenship"?
2. Take a look at one of the online forums for teens to discuss sexuality listed in Appendix D. Can you find a moral or ethical question being discussed explicitly by teens? Can you find one lurking behind what seems to be a different kind of question? Outline a brief plan for how this question could be handled in the classroom.
3. Adolescents are likely to already have some ideas about the ethics of sexual behaviors, and the classroom environment can be a good place for them to express, refine, or revise these thoughts and beliefs. However, this book argues that asking students to come up with their own set of ethics is not enough. Can you think of ways in which the "ethic of care" discussed in Chapter 3 could be introduced in a classroom to help students develop their sense of what constitutes ethical sexual behavior?
4. How important is it to inform students about their rights as a part of sex education? Is it important for adolescents to fully understand their rights? In particular, what about their right to full and accurate information?
5. In what other ways can gender equity, sexual orientation, and gender identity be addressed without creating a "false symmetry"? Give an example of the false symmetry created in discourse about boys and girls.
6. It seems that emotional intimacy, concern for one's partner's views, and the concept that one should endeavor to do no harm have largely been left out of sex ed, but these issues are intimately linked to compassion, which many feel is an important motivating factor behind ethics. Can you think of ways in which we can teach young people skills they need to negotiate pleasurable, ethical sexual intimacy that focus not only on their needs, but the needs of their partners?
7. Discuss the drawbacks of lodging sex ed in fear and shame rather than desire and pleasure. Consider the consequences of a dialogue of fear and shame for individuals, on an interpersonal level, and societally. Are there some acts and behaviors that should bring shame on an individual? Is shame ever useful?

Chapter 4

1. Which attitude do you believe to be the best for a sexuality educator to take: casual or formal? What are the risks and benefits of each approach?
2. How might you handle the issue of privacy and disclosing sensitive information in a high school classroom and why?
3. Write an argument to the school board with regard to why your sexual ethics curriculum should be adopted. Anticipate their objections and counter them.

Chapter 5

1. One common myth about love is the claim that boys are not interested in love, only sex, and that girls are only interested in love and not sex. Carol Cassell (1989) wrote that at the first sign of sexual arousal, women tend to set up a love fantasy. Is there any truth to this myth, or to the ideas behind it? What are some of the things about this myth about love that can send negative or damaging messages to young people?
2. Pick a recent film that depicts sex between friends. What is the message about sex between friends?
3. Looking back on your own adolescence, did you ever experience something that made you feel ashamed about being or feeling sexual? How might we address feelings of shame in ethical sex ed curricula? How can we encourage adolescents to accept confusing feelings such as shame or discomfort with their emerging sexuality?
4. Write one or two scripts that a young person might use as an actual request to do something sexual with another person. Feel free to use a negative example if you like, but at least one script should focus on consent and mirror a positive way of asking one's partner for consent.
5. Argue the idea that nonverbal consent is (or at least can be) adequate and in what circumstances. Feel free to write an additional paragraph analyzing your argument.
6. How might "kinky" sex, BDSM, or role-playing complicate issues of consent? How do safe-words come into play? Do you think teens are aware of this subculture, from the media and their peers? How might this type of sexual activity affect personal autonomy?
7. Masturbation is a controversial topic for sex ed curricula and for parents talking to their teens about sex. Do you think masturbation

should be discussed in the classroom? Should parents talk to children about it? Is it wrong for a mother to give a daughter a vibrator? Is it wrong for a father to joke about "jerking off"?

8. In a sexual ethics curriculum, what place is there for pleasure? What is the relationship of sexual pleasure to sexual ethics? Who can ask for pleasure? Who can't? Why? How does teaching about pleasure universalize the sexual experience for different groups?

Chapter 6

1. According to MacKinnon (2007), whose free speech is protected when pornography is allowed? Whose free speech isn't protected? If you agree that pornography restricts free speech of oppressed people, what should the solution be? In society today, do you think everybody experiences the right to free speech equally?

2. Remember the arguments for free speech, against harm, for protecting rights, and against oppression in porn. Considering these arguments and the opinions expressed above, do you think that porn with disabled people could be considered a positive force in that it includes people with disabilities as potential sexual partners?

3. In the "Without Sanctuary" exhibition of 2000, the New York Historical Society showed photographs taken of Blacks who were lynched in the United States. Brent Staples (2000) wrote of the photographs that the images of people suffering had a numbing effect and even normalized them. By looking at so many in a row we become desensitized and they lose their shocking effect. Is this similar to pornography? Given that much of the porn today is created to be a male fantasy of what women desire or how women might really enjoy sex, does it cause harm to boys and men who then develop distorted views and harm their relationships with girls and women in the future? Is it training in insensitivity?

4. Find two music videos on YouTube that contain Black and White women. Answer these questions about those videos:[1] How are White women and Black women treated differently in the video? Did you see a woman who looked sexually empowered? What did she look like? What was she doing? Did you see a woman who you thought was degraded by her appearance? What did she look like? What was she doing?

5. Compare and contrast the themes, messages, and illustrative language of early rap and today's rap. Do you agree that they have shifted? Why or why not? Suggested early rap songs to research: "The Message" by Grandmaster Flash, "Fight the Power" by Public

Enemy, "Self Destruction" by Stop the Violence Movement, and "UNITY" by Queen Latifah.

6. Think of an example of material consumed by teens which is, at least in some way, sexual. Considering ideas about how the public and the personal are linked, how could this material impact teens on a private and personal level? Consider how "what's outside gets inside." (Examples could include things such as teen vampire dramas, cosmetics with sexually suggestive names, popular swimwear, deodorant commercials, etc.) Discuss a possible counter-discourse for your example.

7. Modern communication tools have changed the nature of privacy and the ease of violating it. How far do you feel one's obligations to maintain another person's privacy extend? Consider sexting as an example.

8. Consider the "emotional labor" of prostitution, and the ways in which sex workers could become alienated from their sense of self or their own bodies. Do you think these are reasonable concepts to ask teens to think about? Are there parallels to their own lives that teens could draw from learning to examine prostitution in this light? Consider Kant's viewpoint regarding using people as a means to an end.

9. Beyond the obvious personal reasons, why is it important for good sexual citizenship for all people to understand what rape is? Consider how rape culture could be explained to teenagers and how rape culture affects people whether or not they have experienced rape. Is it important to discuss rape and sexual violence specifically as a separate discussion in addition to discussions of the importance of consent?

10. Do you agree that including religious teachings from around the world as part of a complete sex ed is a positive step? What makes it difficult to grasp any religion in a single lesson? What would you do in a classroom to convey that there is wide variation in beliefs and practices within any religion?

APPENDIX B

Sample Discussion Questions from the Sexual Ethics for a Caring Society Curriculum (SECS-C)

with Judea Beatrice, Kaelin Farmer, Kelly Graling, Kathryn Hall, Shin-Ye Kim, Kara Lustig, Paula Moebus, and Aleksandra Plocha

Revised from SECS-C for publication

Liking, Loving, and Lusting

Ask adolescents to be philosophers and consider the following:

- Can friends be in love?
- What is love?
- What myths do we believe about love and what evidence do we have that some of these myths are true?
- What happens when sexual desire enters a friendship?
- What is sexual desire without friendship or love?
- Can there be passion for another human being without sexual desire?
- What do all these configurations look like?
- What do you seek in your life?
- Your future?
- What *should* human beings seek in their sexual lives and how might this relate to your future?

Friendship

Consider the ethical qualities of a romantic or sexual relationship in comparison to friendship through these questions:

- Why might it be important to be a friend with someone before you are a boyfriend or girlfriend?
- Does there need to be equality between two people in order for there to be a friendship?
- In what ways is a friend "another self" and in what ways not?
- What challenges a friendship?
- How is friendship different from romantic love?

Consent and Coercion

- Do you need consent to _____? (In this blank and the blanks that follow, insert such things as kiss, touch a breast over the clothes, touch a breast under the clothes, take off your partner's clothes, have sex, etc.)
- Under what circumstances should you ask first?
- Under what circumstances might it be wrong to ask?
- Does asking ruin the fun?
- Do girls and women really want to be swept off their feet?
- Does it matter what gender the initiator is?
- Is it unfair to have different rules for different genders of initiators or different gender pairings?
- How harmful could an unwanted _____ be?
- What's the difference between an unwanted kiss and an unwanted butt grab?
- Does the kind of kiss it is matter?
- Is tacit (unspoken) consent enough?
- How do you know if someone wants you to _____ him or her?
- How can you be sure you're perceiving that person correctly?

Autonomy and Freedom with Regard to Consent

- How much pressure constitutes coercion?
- How much pressure constitutes persuasion?
- Does nagging someone to have sex constitute a coercive kind of pressure?
- Does threatening to break up with the person constitute coercion?
- If a teen believes that she can't get pregnant if she's on top during sex, does that make her consent to have sex invalid? If she knew the risks, she might not have consented to have sex at all.
- What about the developmentally disabled teen? Is his or her consent valid?

Consent and Alcohol

The following scenarios should be imagined with heterosexual as well as lesbian or gay couples:

- If one person has been drinking but the other can't tell if he or she is drunk, can consent be trusted?
- What exactly are the indications of impairment? For example, if a boy asks a girl or a boy to have sex and the other person asks him to use a condom, does asking him to use a condom mean that her or his judgment was not that impaired and that consent to have sex was valid?
- What makes any question an indication that the person's consent is valid?
- Do the circumstances of the drinking make a difference? For example, if someone has spiked the punch so the alcohol level is much higher than a person expects, is the person getting intoxicated against his or her will? (Wertheimer, 2003).
- On the other hand, what if a person purposely drinks in order to feel less inhibited and hook up with someone that night? Does that make the drunken consent more valid? (Wertheimer, 2003).

Society's Messages about Sex

- How does what's outside get inside?
- How does society or culture determine or even produce the way we think about things? Determine our tastes? Get reproduced, supported, and confirmed in the things we say to ourselves?
- How does it mess with our feelings?
- Are there authentic feelings that underlie society's discourses?
- And if there isn't an authentic feeling or thought underneath those things that have become so embedded in who we are, what kinds of counter-discourses can be created?
- How do we resist becoming simple dupes of the cultural moment?

Objectification

- Do heterosexual men and boys benefit from the power that they have to set up or enforce a standard of what is beautiful for females?
- Is there a way for men and boys to ethically respond to this privilege?

- Why do girls themselves enforce standards that are damaging to them? Why might they harm other girls in this way?
- Do we have the right not to have various parts of our bodies looked at? For example, does a woman walking down the street in a form-fitting dress have a right not to be stared at?

Media and Popular Culture

- What do hip hop and rap say about who is a "ho" or a "freak" and why do you suppose they make this distinction?
- What do these labels convey and why did they become popular?
- What do you think is realistic and unrealistic in movie sex? In TV sex?
- Are there different messages for White, Black, Asian, Latino, and other races and ethnicities about sex, body image, and danger in the media?

Sexting

- Is it wrong for friends to indulge in "very personal gossip" about you when they learned the information without violating your rights and they are not violating any confidences in sharing what they know?
- Do people have a right to expect others to keep intimate information about them to themselves?
- Does it make a difference if they told these people the information themselves?
- Is sexting itself wrong? What if it is between two people in a relationship?
- Is a photograph different, or more obscene, than a nude drawing of the person?
- Sexting may be risky, but to what extent is it wrong to give someone else a piece of information about oneself, whether visual or verbal, to keep private?
- What are one's obligations to another person? Do these obligations differ if this person is in a relationship with you when the photograph arrives in your cell phone unbidden?

Pornography

- Is pornography harmful?
- To whom, in what circumstances, and why?

- What is to be done in society about those things that give pleasure to some but harm others?
- Is being insensitive a moral wrong?
- What social and financial influences are in place that promote certain kinds of representations and certain kinds of entertainment?
- What are the alternatives?
- How can citizens ask for more varied and respectful forms of entertainment?

Prostitution

- From Kant's perspective, is the prostitute treating herself or himself as a means to an end, the end being money?
- Is she or he ignoring her or his own autonomy and capabilities?
- Is the person who pays the prostitute for money ignoring her or his humanity? Her or his dignity?
- Is this person treating the prostitute as a means to an end (sexual pleasure)?
- Does the prostitute sell her or his body or a service, and what's the difference?

Religion

In our sexual ethics curriculum, we ask students to study various world religions and their texts and answer the following questions:

- What is the purpose of sex?
- What are the teachings about the body and pleasure?
- When is sex wrong?
- When is sex right?
- Are there specific gender roles associated with sex?

The texts we suggest are the Koran and Sharia law, the Bhagavad Gita, the Kama Sutra, the Bible, the Torah, readings on Buddhism, Hinduism, and Sikhism, as well as anthropological studies of Native American, Hawaiian, and other cultures. We ask students to research their own or another's religion by talking to a leader in their place of worship, talking to their parents, or doing library research.

Sexual Rights

There are so many philosophers in the Western tradition who write about justice and rights that the instructor will have any number to choose from. Indeed, Rawls's (1971) "veil of ignorance" strategy for determining the laws of a society might be an interesting reading with regard to fairness. The reading and discussion would focus on:

- What kinds of laws would a student choose?
- What rights would he or she give to various people in a society?
- Should these laws be decided from a veil of ignorance? That is, prior to knowing what and who one would be in that society?
- What if one were to be born male, female, Black, White, Asian, Latino? Raised to be a Jew, Christian, Muslim, or Buddhist? Have money or not? Be gay, straight, or transsexual?
- What if one were to be plopped down into this society with a set of very particular attributes, attachments, preferences, and desires—what laws would be fair to one's self and to others?

APPENDIX C

Sample Exercises from the Sexual Ethics for a Caring Society Curriculum (SECS-C)

with Judea Beatrice, Kaelin Farmer, Kelly Graling,
Kathryn Hall, Shin-Ye Kim, Kara Lustig,
Paula Moebus, and Aleksandra Plocha

Revised from the SECS-C for publication

Exercise 1: What Is Objectification?

Consider some of these examples:

- A boyfriend and girlfriend are in bed together after sexual activity. He tells her she has a sexy body.
- A young woman is walking down the street and an older man stares at her breasts as she walks by.
- Does your opinion change if it is a young guy whom she had a crush on who stares at her breasts?
- A young woman is walking down the street and an older man grabs her breasts as she walks by.
- A young woman wears a short skirt and a revealing blouse to a party in order to attract a boyfriend.
- A guy takes a girl home from a party and they have sex. He doesn't ask for her phone number because he just wanted to have sex with anyone that night.
- A woman who identifies as queer asks her partner to do a striptease for her.
- A gay man tells another gay guy that he looks like a porn star.

Exercise 2: Sexting Wake-Up Calls

Case 1. In July 2008 an 18-year-old sent sext photographs to her boyfriend. They broke up and her angry ex sought retribution by sending these sexts to his school classmates and friends. This resulted in her suicide by hanging in her bedroom. Although this is a dramatic example, let's talk about:

- Why would she hang herself?
- Why is something that felt fun at first something that later feels shameful or humiliating?

Case 2. A 16-year-old boy faces 7 years in jail for circulating an image of a girlfriend to friends.

- Does it matter if she said it was okay to pass it around?
- Does it count as child porn in your opinion?
- Should there be a punishment? And what should it be?

Case 3. Two Reno teenagers thought they were sending nude photographs of themselves to a 15-year-old boy, but this "boy" turned out to be 45 years old.

- Do you believe the teens?
- Do you think the teens were foolish?
- Does the age of the person they sent the pictures to matter?

Case 4. Now let's think of all the "danger" stories you hear.

- Why are they circulated?
- Do you think they are exaggerations?
- What if, like in the movie *Titanic*, a boy sketched a naked picture of a girl who posed nude for him, and then showed this sketch in an art show at the public library? Would that be different from taking a photo and how?
- Are there understandable reasons why people might want to share naked pictures of themselves with others?

Exercise 3: Rape Myths

In this exercise students can discuss which of these they might possibly agree with while others might argue why they are myths.

1. If a woman is raped while she is drunk, she is at least somewhat responsible for letting things get out of control (Payne, Lonsway, & Fitzgerald, 1999).
2. When women go around wearing low-cut tops or short skirts, they're just asking for trouble (Payne et al., 1999).
3. If a woman goes home with a man she doesn't know, it is her own fault if she is raped (Payne et al., 1999).
4. When a woman is a sexual "tease," eventually she is going to get in trouble (Payne et al., 1999).
5. A rape probably didn't happen if the woman has no bruises or marks (Payne et al., 1999). If the rapist doesn't have a weapon, you really can't call it rape (Payne et al., 1999).
6. If a woman doesn't physically resist sex—even when protesting verbally—it really can't be considered rape (Payne et al., 1999).
7. When men rape, it is because of their strong desire for sex (Payne et al., 1999).
8. When a man is very sexually aroused, he may not even realize that the woman is resisting (Payne et al., 1999).
9. Many women secretly desire to be raped (Payne et al., 1999).
10. Many women find being forced to have sex very arousing (Payne et al., 1999).
11. Some women prefer to have sex forced on them so they don't have to feel guilty about it (Payne et al., 1999).
12. Many so-called rape victims are actually women who had sex and "changed their minds" afterward (Payne et al., 1999).
13. Rape accusations are often used as a way of getting back at men (Payne et al., 1999).
14. A lot of times, women who claim they were raped just have emotional problems (Payne et al., 1999).
15. One reason that women falsely report a rape is that they frequently have a need to call attention to themselves (Burt, 1980).
16. If a woman is willing to "make out" with a guy, then it's no big deal if he goes a little further and has sex (Payne et al., 1999).
17. Rape isn't as big a problem as some feminists would like people to think (Payne et al., 1999).
18. Being raped isn't as bad as being mugged and beaten (Payne et al., 1999).
19. Women tend to exaggerate how much rape affects them (Payne et al., 1999).
20. In reality, women are almost never raped by their boyfriends (Payne et al., 1999).

http://www.endvawnow.org/uploads/browser/files/Rape%20Myths_Questions.pdf

- Discuss why each of these is a myth.
- How does believing each one of these statements contribute to rape culture?

Exercise 4: Stereotypes

1. Imagine you are at a party and one of the following individuals begins to flirt with you. How would the stereotypes associated with this person's social group affect how you perceive him or her as a potential sexual or romantic partner?
   - An individual with a physical disability
   - An African American individual
   - A Latino individual
   - An individual who identifies as bisexual
   - An Asian American individual
   - A White individual
2. How do stereotypes play out in the lives of LGBTQ individuals?
3. Are there any ways in which sexual and gender stereotypes and moral distance between individuals of different groups might contribute to sexual violence?
4. How can we determine if we hold sexual stereotypes and what those sexual stereotypes are?
5. Are we responsible for automatic sexual stereotypic associations that arise in us? Are we responsible for how sexual stereotypes affect our behaviors?
6. Can we internalize sexual stereotypes of our own group? How does that affect us?

Exercise 5: Imagining the Other

This exercise can be used in sex ed classrooms in the process of discussing what rules the class might set up for the conversations they will be having in class. It derives from Rawls's (1971) "veil of ignorance."

If you were _____ you would want there to be a rule that says:

If you had a disability, the rule you would want to have in the classroom that would protect you would be:

If you were African American:

If you were gay:

If you were transgender:

If you had been sexually abused as a child:

If someone you care about has worked as a prostitute:

If you were Asian American:

If you came from a very strictly religious family:

If you came from a liberal family:

If you had been raped:

If you were transgendered:

If you were Jewish:

If you were questioning your sexuality:

If you had been hurt recently by a partner:

If you have low self-esteem about your looks or body:

What general rules might these boil down to?

Exercise 6: Letter to a 12-Year-Old

Write a letter to an imaginary special niece or cousin who is 12 years old and asking you for advice. She has been hanging out with a 15-year-old and would like to "have sex" with this person. What might you say to her in a way that respects her decision to choose for herself and that doesn't sound like a bunch of stereotypes about "waiting for Mr. or Ms. Right"? Would your advice change if this were a male cousin or nephew? What would be the difference in your response if you learned the person she or he has been hanging out with is the same sex? Would there be additional advice?

Exercise 7: Sex Education and Age

The class can break up into groups and be assigned an age group. Each group then needs to decide what this age group needs to know at this age in sex education and justify why this information and not more or less. How does what you believe a student needs to know mesh with what that age group is like developmentally?

Exercise 8: Write Your Own Lesson

The Sexual Ethics for a Caring Society Curriculum website (www.sexandethics.org) encourages students to write their own lessons. There is a community page on which students can write comments about the curriculum and send ideas and sample lesson plans to the author. Try to write your own lesson and send it in. We will consider posting these on the website. Each lesson should feature not only a topic having to do with sex education, for example, STIs or media representations of sexual violence, but also a philosophical and ethical perspective on the issue. For example, for STIs a student could write a lesson on privacy and whether or not one has a responsibility to accurately tell others about the risky sex they may have participated in and when. With regard to TV and sexual violence, a student could write about censorship or stereotypes or the obligation of media to viewers. SECS-C is meant to be a living curriculum and your participation will help the curriculum to address the needs of current students in a changing society.

APPENDIX D

Online Resources

with Kaelin Farmer

WEBSITES FOR TEENS

Advocates for Youth, http://www.advocatesforyouth.org

Advocates for Youth is an organization that works both in the United States and in developing countries with a sole focus on adolescent (ages 14–25) reproductive and sexual health, advocating for a more positive and realistic approach to adolescent sexual health.

Sex, etc., http://www.sexetc.org/

A website that includes a message board, a forum, links, and FAQs for teens, solely written by their peers. Their slogan is "sex education by teens, for teens!"

Scarleteen, http://www.scarleteen.com/

A website written by teens that includes topics such as LGBTQ issues, STIs, a helpline, blogs, polls, and advice. Their slogan is "sex ed for the real world."

Planned Parenthood, http://www.plannedparenthood.org/info-for-teens/

Planned Parenthood's website geared toward teens. It includes links to health information and services, as well as information from teens and doctors about puberty, sex and masturbation, relationships, pregnancy, and LGBTQ issues. It also provides information for parents and educators.

The Kinsey Institute, http://kinseyconfidential.org/

Sexual health information from the Kinsey Institute, which includes blogs, podcasts, reading lists, polls, and links to resources. It also contains articles with a more scientific bent, as well as sections dedicated specifically to pleasure and orgasm, sexual orientation, pregnancy and birth control, health and disease, relationships and love, and sexual assault.

Our Bodies, Ourselves, http://www.ourbodiesourselves.org/

The website for Our Bodies, Ourselves (OBOS), also known as the Boston Women's Health Book Collective (BWHBC), a nonprofit, public-interest women's health education, advocacy, and consulting organization. The site focuses on women's health issues, such as body image, relationships and sexuality, sexual health, reproductive choices, and the politics and history of women's health.

Puberty 101, http://puberty101.com/

A website run by the GovTeen Network for teens and parents to obtain information about a broad range of topics associated with puberty, including separate sections for boys' sexual health, girls' sexual health, STIs, as well as mental health and substance abuse issues.

Go Ask Alice, http://goaskalice.columbia.edu/sexual-and-reproductive-health

The website for Go Ask Alice!, Columbia University's health-question-and-answer resource. This specific section of the site is dedicated to sexual and reproductive health, with a wide variety of issues discussed, ranging from basic male and female sexual health to more taboo topics such as fetishes, pornography, and sex toys.

Maria Talks, www.mariatalks.com

A website run out of Massachusetts that serves as a resource for teens about sexual health questions. Maria identifies as 18 and has a host of "friends" who will answer teen questions.

Sexperience, http://sexperienceuk.channel4.com/

A UK-based website that is primarily a forum for young people to talk about their personal sexual experiences, including videos featuring people talking frankly and occasionally explicitly about their experiences of sex.

Amplify Your Voice, http://www.amplifyyourvoice.org

A project run by Advocates for Youth that focuses on youth activism. Amplify is an online community dedicated to sexual health, reproductive justice, and youth-led grassroots movement building.

Chadzboyz, http://www.chadzboyz.com/

A website dedicated to LGBTQ teens. It includes chat rooms, forums, a Q&A column, polls, and information about safe sex, politics, coming out, and lifestyles. A section for parents is also available, with parental advice and resources provided.

The Asexual Visibility and Education Network, http://www. asexuality.org/home/

An online community and informational resource for the Asexual Visibility and Education Network (AVEN), whose goal is to create public acceptance and discussion of asexuality, and facilitate the growth of an asexual community.

Center for Young Women's Health, http://www. youngwomenshealth.org/

Created by the Center for Young Women's Health at Children's Hospital Boston, this site provides detailed information about sexuality and sexual health, nutrition and fitness, gynecology, general health and development, and emotional health for teen girls, as well as guides for parents.

TeensHealth, http://teenshealth.org/teen/

TeensHealth is part of the KidsHealth family of websites run by the nonprofit Nemours Center for Children's Health Media. The site provides up-to-date information about sexual and emotional health for teens, all of which is reviewed by pediatricians and medical experts regularly.

We're Talking, http://www.pamf.org/teen/

The Palo Alto Medical Foundation's (PAMF) website for teens, "We're Talking," is a source of health information for Bay Area teens 13 to 18 years of age, their parents, and teachers. The website seeks to provide teens with comprehensive, up-to-date, general, sexual, and emotional health information, all of which is reviewed by physicians, social workers, and educators.

Answer (Sex Ed Honestly), http://answer.rutgers.edu/

Answer, formerly known as the Network for Family Life Education, was largely shaped during the 23-year tenure of Susan N. Wilson, MSEd., who currently serves as its senior advisor. It is a national organization dedicated to providing and promoting comprehensive sexuality education to young people and the adults who teach them.

WEBSITES FOR SEX ED POLICY

The Future of Sex Education Project (FoSE), http://www. futureofsexed.org/

The Future of Sex Education Project (FoSE) began in July 2007 when staff from Advocates for Youth, Answer, and SIECUS first met to discuss the future of sex education in the United States. Their aim is to create a national dialogue about the future of sex education and to promote the institutionalization of comprehensive sexuality education in public schools.

On January 9, 2012, they released the *National Sexuality Education Standards: Core Content and Skills, K–12* which was co-written with SIECUS, Answer Sex Ed Honestly, and Advocates for Youth:

http://www.futureofsexed.org/fosestandards.html

The goal of the *National Sexuality Education Standards: Core Content and Skills, K–12* is to provide straightforward guidance on the essential minimum, core content for sexuality education that is age-appropriate for students in grades K–12.

SEICUS Sexuality Information and Education Council of the United States, http://www.siecus.org/index.cfm

In particular, the State Profiles section includes information for Sexuality Education and Abstinence-Only-Until Marriage programs by state:

http://www.siecus.org/index.cfm?fuseaction=Page.
ViewPage&PageID=487

The *Guidelines for Comprehensive Sexuality Education for Kindergarten through 12th Grade,* produced by the National Guidelines Task Force, can be found here:

http://www.siecus.org/_data/global/images/guidelines.pdf

Advocates for Youth

Their website includes information organized by states:

http://www.advocatesforyouth.org/for-professionals/sex-education
-resource-center/766?task=view

In addition, it contains information covering general CSE and AOUM education. *Comprehensive Sex Education: Research and Results* can be found here:

http://www.advocatesforyouth.org/publications/1487?task=view

And the publication *Five Years of AOUM Education: Assessing the Impact* can be found here:

http://www.advocatesforyouth.org/publications/623?task=view

The Guttmacher Institute, http://www.guttmacher.org/

The Guttmacher Institute advances sexual and reproductive health and rights through research, policy analysis, and public education designed to generate new ideas, encourage public debate, and promote policy and program development. They produce a wide range of resources on topics pertaining to sexual and reproductive health, including *Perspectives on Sexual and Reproductive Health, International Perspectives on Sexual and Reproductive Health,* and the *Guttmacher Policy Review.*

Sex Ed Library, http://www.sexedlibrary.org/

A comprehensive online sex ed resource created by SIECUS (the Sexuality Information and Education Council of the United States). They analyze lesson plans from multiple sources that cover such topics as sexual and reproductive health, puberty, abstinence, relationships, sexual orientation, body image, self-esteem, sexually transmitted diseases, HIV/AIDS, unintended pregnancy, and more.

The Kinsey Institute, www.kinseyinstitute.org

The Kinsey Institute website provides information and research about all sex-related topics. It also contains statistics and graphs pertaining to sexuality research such as condom use and age at first intercourse:

http://www.kinseyinstitute.org/resources/FAQ.html

The Centers for Disease Control and Prevention, http://www.cdc.gov/std/default.htm

The CDC's website on sexually transmitted diseases contains up-to-date information, statistics, and graphs about all STDs and STIs, covering all age groups.

The Waxman Report, http://www.apha.org/apha/PDFs/HIV/The_Waxman_Report.pdf

Henry A. Waxman's congressional report on the content of federally funded abstinence-only education programs.

Satcher's (Surgeon General's) Report, http://www.surgeongeneral.gov/library/sexualhealth/index.html

On June 28, 2001, Surgeon General David Satcher unveiled science-based strategies that he said represent an effort to find "common ground" upon which the nation could work to promote sexual health and responsible sexual behavior.

Trenholm et al., 2007, http://www.mathematica-mpr.com/ publications/PDFs/impactabstinence.pdf

Trenholm, Devaney, Fortson, Quay, Wheeler, and Clark's report on the impacts of four Title V, Section 510, abstinence education programs.

The Center for Sexual Pleasure and Health, http://thecsph.org/our-resources/education/curricular-resources

The Center for Sexual Pleasure and Health is designed to provide adults with a safe, physical space to learn about sexual pleasure, health, and advocacy issues. They provide services like one-on-one sexuality consultation services at their offices in Rhode Island, trainings and workshops for professionals, access to sexual health journals, local zines, sexuality-related curricula and learning tools, genital teaching models, and personalized sex toy and sexual aids guidance. They have one of the largest sexual resource and media libraries on the East Coast.

SexLaws.org, http://www.sexlaws.org/

SexLaws.org provides a database of information regarding statutory rape, age of consent, sexual assault, and any similar laws in the United States. Their goal is to provide up-to-date information for each state, and even specific cities where the laws vary. Their website provides links to current news articles, government reports, and a Q&A board that addresses questions regarding the legal issues of a variety of sexual topics.

Notes

Chapter 5

1. The writing on Aristotle in this section comes in part from the Sexual Ethics for a Caring Society Curriculum (SECS-C) that is currently available online at www.sexandethics.org. It also relies on explanations from Michael Sandel's Harvard University ethics course (www.justiceharvard.com) as well as a curriculum available online from ethics professor Robert Cavalier at Carnegie Mellon (http://www.phil.cmu.edu/Cavalier/80130/part1/sect1/Aristotle.html).

2. Screen names have been changed.

3. I want to acknowledge Kara Lustig's leading voice in the curriculum section on age of consent. Her thinking is clearly reflected in this section as well.

4. Paula Moebus was the lead author on the SECS-C's section on shame and so has influenced the discussion in this section.

Chapter 6

1. Bettina Love wrote the first draft of the lesson on music and lyrics for the SECS-C, the online curriculum that accompanies this book. The material in this chapter draws from that lesson.

2. Kara Lustig, a PhD student in Clinical Psychology at UMass Boston, took the lead in this section of the SECS-C online curriculum. Her work is reflected here.

3. Judea Beatrice wrote the first draft of this section for our Sexual Ethics Curriculum, and her influence is reflected in the information here.

Appendix A

1. The questions about hip hop and rap were initially written by Bettina Love, Department of Elementary and Social Studies Education, University of Georgia, Athens, GA, before the research group worked on them for the curriculum.

References

Abraham, L. (2011, November 16). Teaching good sex. *New York Times*. Retrieved at http://www.nytimes.com/2011/11/20/magazine/teaching-good-sex.html

Administration for Children and Families and the Department of Health and Human Services. (2007). *Review of comprehensive sex education curricula*. Retrieved at http://www.abstinence.net/pdf/contentmgmt/Review_of_Comprehensive_Sex_Education_Curricula-2.pdf

Advocates for Youth (updated by Keefe, M.). (2007). *The history of federal abstinence only funding*. Retrieved at http://www.advocatesforyouth.org/publications/429?task=view

Allen, A. L. (1988). *Uneasy access: Privacy for women in a free society*. Totowa, N.J: Rowman & Littlefield.

Allen, L. (2003). Girls want sex, boys want love: Resisting dominant discourses of (hetero)sexuality. *Sexualities, 6*, 215–236. doi:10.1177/1363460703006002004

Allen, L. (2004). Beyond the birds and the bees: Constituting a discourse of erotics in sexuality education. *Gender and Education, 16*(2), 151–167. doi:10.1080/09540250310001690555

Allen , L. (2005). "Say everything": Exploring young people's suggestions for improving sexuality education. *Sex Education, 5*(4), 389–404.

Allen, L. (2007a). Doing "it" differently: Relinquishing the disease and pregnancy prevention focus in sexuality education. *British Journal of Sociology of Education, 28*(5), 575–588.

Allen, L. (2007b). "Pleasurable pedagogy": Young people's ideas about teaching "pleasure" in sexuality education. *21st Century Society, 2*, 249–264.

Allen, L. (2008). "They think you shouldn't be having sex anyway": Young people's suggestions for improving sexuality education content. *Sexualities, 11*(5), 573–594.

American Psychological Association Task Force on the Sexualization of Girls. (2007). *Report of the APA task force on the sexualization of girls*. Washington, DC: American Psychological Association. Retrieved from http://www.apa.org/PI/women/programs/girls/report.aspx

Aristotle. (n. d.). *The Nicomachean ethics* (Book 8, Ch. 8). (W. D. Ross, trans., 1958). Retrieved from http://classics.mit.edu/Aristotle/nicomachaen.8.viii.html

Ashcraft, C. (2006). "Girl, you better go get you a condom": Popular culture and teen sexuality as resources for critical multicultural curriculum. *Teachers College Record, 108*(10), 2145–2186.

Augustine. (n. d.). *Confessions.* (A. C. Outler, Trans., 1955). Philadelphia: Westminster Press.

Baber, K. M., & Murray, C. I. (2001). A postmodern feminist approach to reaching human sexuality. *Family Relations, 50*(1), 23–33.

Badash, D. (2012, August 19). US Congressman: Rape victims' bodies 'shut down' pregnancies automatically, no need for abortion. *The New Civil Rights Movement.* Retrieved from http://thenewcivilrightsmovement.com/us-congressman-rape-victims-bodies-shut-down-pregnancies-automatically-no-need-for-abortion/politics/2012/08/19/46974

Bailey, J., & McCafferty, J. (2004). *Sex, puberty, and all that stuff: A guide to growing up.* Hauppauge, NY: Barron's Educational Series.

Barth, R. P. (2004). *Reducing the risk: Building skills to prevent pregnancy, STD & HIV* (4th ed.). Scotts Valley, CA: ETR Associates.

Bartky, S. L. (1990). *Femininity and domination: Studies in the phenomenology of oppression.* New York: Routledge.

Bay-Cheng, L. Y. (2003). The trouble of teen sex: The construction of adolescent sexuality through school-based sexuality education. *Sex Education, 3*(1), 61–74.

Berkowitz, M., & Gibbs, J. (1983). Measuring the developmental features of moral discussion. *Merrill-Palmer Quarterly, 29,* 399–410.

Beil, L. (2007, July 18). Abstinence education faces an uncertain future. *New York Times.* Retrieved from http://www.nytimes.com/2007/07/18/education/18abstain.html

Blatt, M., & Kohlberg, L. (1975). The effects of classroom moral discussion upon children's level of moral judgment. *Journal of Moral Education, 4,* 129–161.

Blum, L. (2004). Stereotypes and stereotyping: A moral analysis. *Philosophical Papers, 33*(3), 251–298.

Blum, L. (forthcoming). False racial symmetries in "Far from Heaven" and elsewhere. In S. Wolf & C. Grau (Eds.), *Understanding love through philosophy, film, and fiction.* New York: Oxford University Press.

Boonstra, H. (2004). Comprehensive approach needed to combat sexually transmitted infections among youth. *The Guttmacher Report on Public Policy, 7*(1), 3–4, 13.

Boonstra, H. (2010). *Sex education: Another big step forward—And a step back.* Retrieved from the Guttmacher Institute website: http://www.guttmacher.org/pubs/gpr/13/2/gpr130227.html

Brick, P., & Taverner, B. (2001). *Positive images: Teaching abstinence, contraception, and sexual health.* Morristown, NJ: Planned Parenthood of Greater Northern New Jersey.

Brown, J. D., Halpern, C. T., & L'Engle, K. L. (2005). Mass media as a sexual super peer for early maturing girls. *Journal of Adolescent Health, 36*(5), 420–427.

Brown, J. D., L'Engle, K. L., Pardun, C. J., Guo, G., Kenneavy, K., & Jackson, C. (2006). Sexy media matter: Exposure to sexual content in music, movies, television, and magazines predicts black and white adolescents' sexual behavior. *Pediatrics, 117,* 1018–1027.

Brown, L. K., & Brown, M. (2000). *What's the big secret?: Talking about sex with girls and boys.* Boston, MA: Little, Brown and Company.

Brown, L. M., Lamb, S., & Tappan, M. (2009). *Packaging boyhood: Saving our sons from superheros, slackers, and other media stereotypes*. New York: St. Martin's Press.

Brown, S., & Taverner, B. (2001). *Streetwise to sex-wise: Sexuality education for high-risk youth* (2th ed.). Morristown, NJ: Planned Parenthood of Northern New Jersey.

Brückner, H., & Bearman, P. (2005). After the promise: The STD consequences of adolescent virginity pledges. *Journal of Adolescent Health, 36*(4), 271–278.

Burt, M. R. (1980). Cultural myths and supports for rape. *Journal of Personality and Social Psychology, 38*(2), p. 217–230.

Buston, K., & Hart, G. (2001). Heterosexism and homophobia in Scottish school sex education: Exploring the nature of the problem. *Journal of Adolescence, 24*, 95–109. doi:10.1006/jado.2000.0366

Cagampang, H., Barth, R., Korpi, M., & Kirby, D. (1997). Education now and babies later (ENABL): Life history of a campaign to postpone sexual involvement. *Family Planning Perspectives, 29*(3), 109–114.

Capellanus, A. (n. d.). *The art of courtly love*. (J. J. Parry, Trans., 1990). New York: Columbia University Press.

Card, C. (1996). Against marriage and motherhood. *Hypatia, 11*(3), 1–23.

Carmody, M. (2005). Ethical erotics: Rethinking anti-rape education. *Sexualities, Journal of Culture and Society, 8*(4), 469–485.

Cassell, C. (1989). *Swept away: Why women confuse love and sex*. New York: Simon & Schuster.

Cavalier, R. (2011). *Online guide to ethics and moral philosophy*. Retrieved from http://www.phil.cmu.edu/Cavalier/80130/part1/sect1/Aristotle.html

Centers for Disease Control (CDC). (2011). *Teenagers in the United States: Sexual activity, contraceptive use, and childbearing, 2006–2010 national survey of family growth series*. Washington, DC: US Department of Health and Human Services. Retrieved from http://www.cdc.gov/nchs/data/nhsr/nhsr036.pdf

Chastity.org. (n.d.a). *FAQ: What's wrong with just hooking up with a girl?* Retrieved from http://www.chastity.org/chastity-qa/how-far-too-far/hooking-up/whats-wrong-with-just

Chastity.org. (n.d.b). *FAQ: Isn't being chaste the same thing as being a prude?* Retrieved from http://www.chastity.org/chastity-qa/how-stay-pure/purity-daily-life/isnt-being-chast

Christman, J. (2009). Autonomy in moral and political philosophy. In E. N. Zalta (Ed.), *The Stanford encyclopedia of philosophy* (Spring 2011 ed.) Retrieved from http://plato.stanford.edu/archives/spr2011/entries/autonomy-moral/

Cole, J., & Tiegreen, A. (2009). *Asking about sex and growing up: A question-and-answer book for boys and girls*. New York: HarperCollins.

Collins, C., Alagiri, P., Summers, T., & Morin, S. F. (2002). *Abstinence only vs. comprehensive sex education: What are the arguments? What is the evidence?* San Francisco: Center for AIDS Prevention Studies (CAPS), University of California, San Francisco.

Collins, P. H. (2000). *Black feminist thought: Knowledge, consciousness, and the politics of empowerment* (2nd ed.). New York: Routledge.

Collins, P. H. (2004). *Black sexual politics: African Americans, gender, and the new racism*. New York: Routledge.

Collins, R. L., Elliott, M. N., Berry, S. H., Kanouse, D. E., & Hunter, S. B. (2003). Entertainment television as a healthy sex educator: The impact of condom-efficacy information in an episode of "Friends." *Pediatrics, 112*(5), 1115–1121.

Cook, B. (2006). *Choosing the best journey.* Atlanta, GA: Choosing the Best Publishing.

Crosson-Tower, C. (2010). *Understanding child abuse and neglect.* Boston: Allyn & Bacon.

Curtler, H. M. (2004). *Ethical argument: Critical thinking in ethics.* New York: Oxford University Press.

Dailard, C. (2001, February). Sexuality education: Politicians, parents, teachers and teens. *Guttmacher Report on Public Policy,* pp. 9–12

Dailard, C. (2005). Administration tightens rules for abstinence education grants. *Guttmacher Report on Public Policy.* Retrieved from http://www.guttmacher.org/pubs/tgr/08/4/gr080413.html

De Tocqueville, A. (1899). *Democracy in America.* (Henry Reeves, Trans.). Retrieved from http://xroads.virginia.edu/~HYPER/DETOC/1_ch15.htm (Original work published 1835)

DeCew, J. (2008). Privacy. In E. N. Zalta (Ed.), *The Stanford encyclopedia of philosophy* (Fall 2008 ed.). Retrieved from http://plato.stanford.edu/archives/fall2008/entries/privacy/

Dewey, J. (1909). *Moral principles in education.* Boston: Houghton Mifflin Company.

Dines, G. (2010). *Pornland: How pornography has hijacked our sexuality.* Boston: Beacon Press.

Diorio, J., & Munro, J. (2003). What does puberty mean to adolescents? Teaching and learning about bodily development. *Sex Education, 3*(2), 119–131.

Donnerstein. E., & Smith, S. (2001). Sex in the media: Theory, influences, and solutions. In D. G. Singer & J. L. Singer (Eds.), *Handbook of children and the media* (pp. 289–307). Thousand Oaks, CA: Sage.

Dubiecki, D. (Producer), & Reitman, J. (Director). (2004). *Consent.* United States: Dubiecki Films. Retrieved from http://www.youtube.com/watch?v=5B5NMN7GBA4

Dutton, D. G., & Aron, A. P. (1974). Some evidence for heightened sexual attraction under conditions of high anxiety. *Journal of Personality and Social Psychology, 30*(4), 510–517.

Eaton, A. W. (2007). A sensible anti-porn feminism. *Ethics, 117,* 674–715.

Elia, J. P. (2000). Democratic sexuality education: A departure from sexual ideologies and traditional schooling. *Journal of Sex Education & Therapy, 25*(2–3), 122–129.

Elia, J. P., & Eliason, M. (2010). Discourses of exclusion: Sexuality education's silencing of sexual others. *Journal of LGBT Youth, 7,* 29–48.

Evans, D. T. (1993). *Sexual citizenship: The material construction of sexualities.* New York: Routledge.

Farley, M. (2003). *Prostitution, trafficking, and traumatic stress.* Binghamton, NY: Hayworth Press.

Fields, J. (2005). "Children having children": Race, innocence, and sexuality education. *Social Problems, 52*(4), 549–571.

Fields, J. (2008). *Risky lessons: Sex education and social inequality.* Piscataway, NJ: Rutgers University Press.

Finders, M. (1999). Raging hormones: Stories of adolescence and implications for teacher preparation. *Journal of Adolescent & Adult Literacy, 42,* 252–263.

Fine, M. (1988). Sexuality, schooling, and adolescent females: The missing discourse of desire. *Harvard Educational Review, 58,* 29–53.

Fine, M., & McClelland, S. (2006). Sexuality education and desire: Still missing after all these years. *Harvard Educational Review, 76,* 297–338.

Fisher, C. M. (2009). Queer youth experiences with Abstinence-Only-Until-Marriage sexuality education: "I can't get married so where does that leave me?" *Journal of LGBT Youth, 6,* 61–79.

Foshee, V., & Langwick, S. (2010). *Safe dates: An adolescent dating abuse prevention curriculum* (2nd ed.). Center City, MN: Hazelden Publishing.

Foucault, M. (1990). *The history of sexuality: An introduction* (Vol. 1). New York: Vintage Books.

Fredrickson, B. L., & Roberts, T. A. (1997). Objectification theory: Toward understanding women's lived experiences and mental health risks. *Psychology of Women Quarterly, 21*(2), 173–206.

Freire, P. (1970). *Pedagogy of the oppressed.* New York: Basic Books.

Fried, C. (1970). *An anatomy of values.* Cambridge, MA: Harvard University Press.

Friedman, M. (2003). *Autonomy, gender, and politics.* New York: Oxford University Press.

Froyum, C. M. (2009). Making "good girls": Sexual agency in the sexuality education of low income black girls. *Culture, Health & Sexuality, 12,* 59–82. doi:10.1080/13691050903272583

Gentile, D. A., & Sesma, A. (2003). Developmental approaches to understanding media effects on individuals. In D. A. Gentile (Ed.), *Media violence and children: A complete guide for parents and professionals* (pp. 19–38). Westport, CT: Ablex.

George, R. P., & Moschella, M. (2011, October 18). Does sex ed undermine parental rights? *New York Times.* Retrieved from http://www.nytimes.com/2011/10/19/opinion/does-sex-ed-undermine-parental-rights.html

Gill, R. (2012). Media, empowerment and the "sexualization of culture" debates. *Sex Roles 66*(11–12), 736–745. doi:10.1007/s11199-011-0107-1

Gilligan, C. (1982). *In a different voice: Psychological theory and women's development.* Cambridge, MA: Harvard University Press.

Giroux, H., & Penna, A. (1983). Social education in the classroom: The dynamics of the hidden curriculum. In H. Giroux & D. Purpel (Eds.), *The hidden curriculum and moral education* (pp. 100–121). Berkeley, CA: McCutchan Publishing.

Gitchel, S., & Foster L. (2005). *Let's talk about S-E-X: A guide for kids 9 to 12 and their parents.* Excelsior, MN: The Book Peddlers.

Glick, P., & Fiske, S. T. (1996). The ambivalent sexism inventory: Differentiating hostile and benevolent sexism. *Journal of Personality and Social Psychology, 70,* 491–512. doi:10.1037/0022-3514.70.3.491

Goldfarb, E. S., & Casparian, E. M. (2000). *Our whole lives: Sexuality education for grades 10–12.* Boston: Unitarian Universalist Association.

Gollwitzer, P. M., Earle, W. B., & Stephan, W. G. (1982). Affect as a determinant of egotism: Residual excitation and performance attributions. *Journal of Personality and Social Psychology, 43*(4), 702–709.

Greene, V. S. (1999). *Television viewing, perceptions of advertising's influence and appearance-related concerns* (Unpublished manuscript). University of Massachusetts, Amherst.

Gresle-Favier, C. (2010). The legacy of abstinence-only discourses and the place of pleasure in US discourses on teenage sexuality. *Sex Education, 10*(4), 413–422.

Gutmann, A. (1987). *Democratic education*. Princeton, N.J: Princeton University Press.

Guttmacher Institute (2007). *Review of comprehensive sex education curricula commissioned by the administration for children and families*. Retrieved from http://www.guttmacher.org/media/evidencecheck/2007/07/01/AdvisoryOnACFsexEdReview.pdf

Hall, G. S. (1904). *Adolescence: Its psychology and its relations to physiology, anthropology, sociology, sex, crime, religion and education*. New York: D. Appleton & Company.

Halstead, J. M., & Reiss, M. J. (2003). *Values in sex education: From principles to practice*. New York: RoutledgeFalmer.

Harris, R. H., & Emberley, M. (2009). *It's perfectly normal: Changing bodies, growing up, sex, and sexual health (the family library)*. Somerville, MA: Candlewick Press.

Harrison, L., Hillier, L., & Walsh, J. (1996). Teaching for a positive sexuality: Sounds good, but what about fear, embarrassment, risk and the "forbidden" discourse of desire? In L. Lasky & C. Beavis (Eds.), *Schooling and sexualities: Teaching for a positive sexuality* (pp. 69–82). Geelong, Australia: Deakin University Press.

Hawkes, G. (2004). *Sex and pleasure in western culture*. Cambridge, UK: Polity Press.

Henneman, T. (2005, August 16). Sex, lies, and teenagers. *Advocate, 944*, 58–59.

Hochschild, A. R. (1983). *The managed heart: Commercialization of human feeling*. Berkeley: University of California Press.

Holland, J., Ramazanoglu, C., Sharpe, S., & Thomson, R. (1998). *The male in the head: Young people, heterosexuality, and power*. London: Tufnell Press.

Howell, J. W. (Ed.). (2007). *The Greenwood encyclopedia of love, courtship, and sexuality throughout history*. Wesport, CT: Greenwood Press.

Huston, A. C., Wartella, E., & Donnerstein, E. (1998). *Measuring the effects of sexual content in the media*. Menlo Park, CA: Kaiser Family Foundation.

Hyman, I. (2010). Is this love or too much caffeine? Misattributions of arousal strengthen relationships. *Mental Mishaps*. Retrieved from http://www.psychologytoday.com/blog/mental-mishaps/201004/is-love-or-too-much-caffeine-misattributions-arousal-strengthen-relations.

Irvine, J. M. (2002). *Talk about sex: The battles over sex education in the United States*. Berkeley: University of California Press.

Jackson, S., & Scott, S. (1997). Gut reactions to matters of the heart: Reflections on rationality, irrationality, and sexuality. *Sociological Review, 45*(4), 551–575.

Jackson, S., & Weatherall, A. (2010). The (im)possibilities of feminist school based sexuality education. *Feminism & Psychology, 20*, 166–185.

Jakobsen, J. R., & Pellegrini, A. (2008). *Secularisms*. Durham, NC: Duke University Press.

James, L., Brown, C., & Dean, E. (2009). *Back to the crib* (Recorded by J. Santana featuring C. Brown). On *Born to lose, built to win* (CD). Skull Gagne & Def Jam.

Janssen, D. F. (2009). Sex as development: Curriculum, pedagogy and critical inquiry. *The Review of Education, Pedagogy, & Cultural Studies, 31*(1), 2–28.

Jemmott, L. S., Jemmott, J. B., & McCaffree, K. A. (1996). *Be proud! Be responsible!: Strategies to empower youth to reduce their risk for HIV infection. Curriculum manual.* New York: Select Media.

John Birch Society. *Political research associates.* (2010) Retrieved January 5, 2012 from http://www.publiceye.org/tooclose/jbs.html

Kahn, A. S., Jackson, J., Kully, C., Badger, K., & Halvorsen, J. (2003). Calling it rape: Differences in experiences of women who do or do not label their sexual assault as rape. *Psychology of Women Quarterly, 27*(3), 233–242.

Kaiser Family Foundation. (2000). *Sexuality education in America: A view from inside the nation's classrooms; Kaiser Family Foundation survey of parents, teachers, principals, and students.* Menlo Park, CA: Author.

Kaiser Family Foundation (2007). *Children, parents, and media: A Kaiser Family Foundation survey.* Retrieved from http://www.kff.org/entmedia/upload/7638.pdf

Kaiser Family Foundation. (2011, January). *Sexual health of teenagers and young adults in the United States.* Menlo Park, CA: Author. Retrieved from http://www.kff.org/womenshealth/upload/3040-05-2.pdf

Kant, I. (1930). *Lecture on ethics.* (L. Infield, Trans.). Indianapolis, IN: Hackett. (Original work published 1780)

Kant, I. (1996). *Groundwork of the metaphysics of morals.* (M. J. Gregor, Trans.). Cambridge, UK: Cambridge University Press. (Original work published 1785).

Kehily, M. J. (2002). Sexing the subject: Teachers, pedagogies and sex education. *Sex Education, 2*(3), 215–231.

Kendall, N. (2008a). Introduction to special issue: The state(s) of sexuality education in America. *Sexuality Research and Social Policy, 5*(2), 1–11.

Kendall, N. (2008b). Sexuality education in an abstinence-only era: A comparative case study of two U.S. states. *Sexuality Research & Social Policy, 5*(2), 23–44. doi:10.1525/srsp.2008.5.2.23

Kiely, E. (2005). Where is the discourse of desire? Deconstructing the Irish Relationships and Sexuality Education (RSE) resource materials. *Irish Educational Studies, 24*(2–3), 253–266.

Kilbourne, J. (1979). *Killing us softly: Advertising's image of women* [Motion picture]. Available from Media Education Foundation, 60 Masonic Street, Northampton, MA 01060

Kilbourne, J. (1995). *Slim hopes: Advertising & the obsession with thinness* [Motion picture]. Available from Media Education Foundation, 60 Masonic Street, Northampton, MA 01060.

Kirby, D. (2001). *Emerging answers: Research findings on programs to reduce teen pregnancy.* Washington, D.C.: The National Campaign to Prevent Teen Pregnancy.

Kirby, D. (2002). *Do abstinence-only programs delay the initiation of sex among young people and reduce teen pregnancy?* Washington, DC: The National Campaign to Prevent Teen Pregnancy.

Kirby, D. (2007). *Emerging answers 2007: Research finding on programs to reduce teen pregnancy and sexually transmitted diseases.* Washington, DC: The National Campaign to Prevent Teen and Unplanned Pregnancy.

Kohlberg, L. (1981). *The philosophy of moral development: Moral stages and the idea of justice.* San Francisco: Harper & Row.

Kohlberg, L., Lieberman, M., Higgins, A., & Power, C. (1982). The just community school and its curriculum: Implications for the future. *Moral Education Forum, 6*(4), 31–42.

Krauth, J. (2003). *WAIT Training.* Greenwood Village, CO: Abstinence and Relationship Training Center.

Lamb, S. (1997). Sex education as moral education: Teaching for pleasure, about fantasy, and against abuse. *Journal of Moral Education, 26*(3), 301–306.

Lamb, S. (2002). *The secret lives of girls: What good girls really do—Sex play, aggression, and their guilt.* New York: Free Press.

Lamb, S. (2006). *Sex, therapy, and kids: Addressing their concerns through talk and play.* New York: Oxford University Press.

Lamb, S. (2010). Towards a sexual ethics curriculum: Bringing philosophy and society to bear on individual development. *Harvard Educational Review, 80*(1), 81–105.

Lamb, S., Beatrice, J., Graling, K., Kim, S., Love, B., Lustig, K., . . . Plocha, A. (2012). *Sexual ethics for a caring society: Curriculum (SECS-C).* Retrieved from http://sexandethics.org

Lamb, S., & Brown, L. M. (2007). *Packaging girlhood: Rescuing our daughters from marketers' schemes.* New York: St. Martin's Griffin.

Lamb, S., & Coakley, M. (1993). Normal childhood sexual play and games: Differentiating play from abuse. *Child Abuse and Neglect, 17,* 515–526.

Lamb, S., Graling, K., & Lustig, K. (2011). Stereotypes in four current AOUM curricula: Good girls, good boys, and the new gender equality. *American Journal of Sexuality Education, 6*(4), 360–380.

Lamb, S., Lustig, K., & Graling, K. (in press). The use and misuse of pleasure in sex ed curricula. *Sex Education.*

Landry, D., Kaeser, L., & Richards, C. (1999). Abstinence promotion and the provision of information about contraception in public school sexuality education policies. *Family Planning Perspectives, 31*(6), 280–286.

LeCroy & Milligan Associates. (2003). *Final report: Arizona abstinence-only education program evaluation, 1998–2003.* Phoenix: Arizona Department of Health Services, Office of Women's and Children's Health.

Lensky, H. (1990). Beyond plumbing and prevention: Feminist approaches to sex education. *Gender and Education, 2*(2), 217–230. doi:10.1080/0954025900020206

Lesko, N. (2010). Feeling abstinent? Feeling comprehensive? Touching the affects of sexuality curricula. *Sex Education, 10*(3), 281–297. doi:10.1080/14681811.2010.491633

Levin, D. E., & Kilbourne, J. (2008). *So sexy so soon: The new sexualized childhood and what parents can do to protect their kids.* New York: Ballantine Books.

Lewis, H. B. (1971). *Shame and guilt in neurosis.* New York: International Universities Press.

Lowry, E. B. (1914). *Teaching sex hygeine in the public schools.* Chicago: Forbes and Co.

Luker, K. (2006). *When sex goes to school: Warring views on sex—and sex education—since the sixties.* New York: Norton.

MacIntyre, A. (1981). *After virtue.* Notre Dame, IN: Notre Dame University Press.

MacKinnon, C. A. (1989). *Toward a feminist theory of the state*. Cambridge, MA: Harvard University Press.

MacKinnon, C. A. (2007). Pornography, civil rights, and speech. In L. L. O'Toole, J. R. Schiffman, & M. Edwards (Eds.), *Gender violence: Interdisciplinary perspectives* (2nd ed., pp. 374–388). New York: New York University Press.

Manlove, J. M., Romano-Papillo, A., & Ikramullah, E. (2004). *Not yet: Programs to delay first sex among teens*. Washington, DC: National Campaign to Prevent Teen Pregnancy.

Marshall, S. E. (1999). Bodyshopping: The case of prostitution. *Journal of Applied Philosophy, 16*(2), 139–150.

Marx, K., Engels, F., Moore, S., & Aveling, E. B. (1876/1992). *Das Kapital: A critique of political economy*. Norwalk, CT: Easton Press.

Mast, C. K. (1986). *Sex respect, the option of true sexual freedom: A public health manual for teachers*. Bradley, IL: Respect for Sexuality.

Mill, J. S. (1859/2008). *On liberty*. New Orleans, LA: Megalodon Entertainment.

Mill, J. S. (1867). *Utilitarianism* (4th ed.). London, UK: Longmans, Green, Reader, and Dyer.

Mitchell, K. J., Finkelhor, D., Jones, L. M., & Wolak, J. (2011). Prevalence and characteristics of youth sexting: A national study. *Pediatrics*, doi:10.1542/peds.2011-1730

Moorti, S. (2002). *Color of rape: Gender and race in television's public spheres*. Albany: State University of New York Press.

Moran, J. P. (2000). *Teaching sex: The shaping of adolescence in the 20th century*. Cambridge, MA: Harvard University Press.

Noddings, N. (2002). *Educating moral people: A caring alternative to character education*. New York: Teachers College Press.

Nossiter, A. (1996, September 27). 6-year-old's sex crime: Innocent peck on cheek. *New York Times*. Retrieved from http://www.nytimes.com/1996/09/27/us/6-year-old-s-sex-crime-innocent-peck-on-cheek.html?pagewanted=all&src=pm

Nussbaum, M. C. (1995). Objectification. *Philosophy & Public Affairs, 24*, 249–291.

Nussbaum, M. C. (1999). *Sex and social justice*. New York: Oxford University Press.

Nussbaum, M. C. (2001). *The fragility of goodness: Luck and ethics in Greek tragedy and philosophy*. New York: Cambridge University Press.

Obama, B. (2009). Inaugural address. In J. T. Woolley & G. Peters (Eds.), *The American presidency project*. Retrieved March 17, 2009 from http://www.presidency.ucsb.edu/ws/index.php?pid=44

O'Neill, O. (1985). Between consenting adults. *Philosophy and Public Affairs, 14*(3), 252–277.

Pateman, C. (1988). *The sexual contract*. Stanford, CA: Stanford University Press.

Paul, A. M. (1998, May 1). Where bias begins: The truth about stereotypes. *Psychology Today*. Retrieved from http://www.psychologytoday.com/articles/199805/where-bias-begins-the-truth-about-stereotypes?

Payne, D. L., Lonsway, K. A., & Fitzgerald, L. F. (1999). Rape myth acceptance: Exploration of its structure and its measurement using the Illinois Rape Myth Acceptance Scale. *Journal of Research in Personality, 33*, 27–68.

Phelps, S., & Gray, L. (2001). *A.C. Green's game plan abstinence program*. Golf, IL: Project Reality.

Phelps, S. (2006). *Aspire: Live your life. Be free.* Arlington Heights, IL: A&M Resources.

Piaget, J. (1948). *The moral judgement of the child.* Glencoe, IL: Free Press.

Plato (n. d.). *Symposium.* (B. Jowett, Trans., 1952). Retrieved from http://classics. mit.edu/Plato/symposium.html

Positive Choice Program. (n.d.). A through H and the positive choice program. Retreived from http://www.positive-choice.org/a-h.htm

Rasmussen, M. (2004). Wounded identities, sex and pleasure: "Doing it" at school. NOT! *Discourse: Studies in the Cultural Politics of Education, 25*(4), 445–458.

Rasmussen, M. (2010). Secularism, religion and 'progressive' sex education. *Sexualities, 13*(6), 699–712. doi:10.1177/1363460710384558

Rawls, J. (1971). *Theory of justice.* Cambridge, MA: Harvard University Press.

Redman, P. (1994). Shifting ground: Rethinking sexuality education. In D. Epstein (Ed.), *Challenging lesbian and gay inequalities in education* (pp. 98–117). Buckingham, UK: Open University Press.

Reis, B., et. al. (2011). *11/12 F.L.A.S.H.: Family Life and Sexual Health High School.* Retrieved June 19, 2012, from http://www.kingcounty.gov/healthservices/ health/personal/famplan/educators/HighSchool.aspx

Rose, S. (2005). Going too far? Sex, sin and social polity. *Social Forces, 84,* 1207–1232.

Rousseau, J. (1762). *Emile, or On Education.* (A. Bloom, Trans., 1979). New York: Basic Books.

Russell, G. M., & Bohan, J. S. (1999). Implications for public policy. In J. S. Bohan & G. M. Russell (Eds.), *Conversations about psychology and sexual orientation* (pp. 139–164). New York: New York University.

Saltz, G., & Cravath, L. A. (2008). *Amazing you!: Getting smart about your private parts.* New York: Puffin Books.

Sandel, M. J. (2009). *Justice: What's the right thing to do?* New York: Farrar, Straus, & Giroux.

Sandel, M. J. (2011). *Harvard University's Justice with Michael Sandel.* Retrieved from http://www.justiceharvard.org

Santelli, J., Ott, M. A., Lyon, M., Rogers, J., Summers, D., & Schleifer, R. (2006). Abstinence and abstinence-only education: A review of U.S. policies and programs. *Journal of Adolescent Health, 38*(1), 72–81.

Satcher, D. (2001). *The surgeon general's call to action to promote sexual health and responsible sexual behavior.* Retrieved from http://www.surgeongeneral.gov/ library/sexualhealth/call.pdf

Satz, D. (1995). Markets in women's sexual labor. *Ethics, 106,* 63–85.

Scarleteen. (2003). *Topic: Sexual harassment at the Oscars?* Retrieved from http://www. scarleteen.com/cgi-bin/forum/ultimatebb.cgi?ubb=get_topic;f=8;t=000665;p=0

Schaffner, L. (2005). Capacity, consent, and the construction of adulthood. In E. Bernstein & L. Schaffner (Eds.), *Regulating sex: The politics of intimacy and identity* (pp. 189–205). New York: Routledge.

Schemo, D. J. (2001, June 29). Surgeon general's report calls for sex education beyond abstinence. *New York Times.* Retrieved from http://www.nytimes. com/2001/06/29/us/surgeon-general-s-report-calls-for-sex-education-beyond-abstinence.html?pagewanted=all&src=pm

Schwartz, A. (2005). *Under the covers: The complexities of sex role stereotyping in class-room practices of three Ontario sexuality education teachers* (Doctoral dissertation). Retrieved from ProQuest Digital Dissertations. (AAT MR11404)

Sethna, C. (2010). Animal sex: Purity education and the naturalization of the abstinence agenda. *Sex Education, 10*(3), 267–279.

Shih, M., Pittinsky, T. L., & Ambady, N. (1999). Stereotype susceptibility: Iden-tity salience and shifts in quantitative performance. *Psychological Science, 10*, 80–83.

SIECUS. (2008). *National opponents of comprehensive sexuality education.* Retrieved from http://www.communityactionkit.org/index.cfm?pageId=920

Staples, B. (2000, April 9). Editorial observer: The perils of growing com-fortable with evil. *New York Times.* Retrieved from http://www.nytimes.com/2000/04/09/opinion/editorial-observer-the-perils-of-growing-comfortable-with-evil.html

Steele, C. M. (1997). A threat in the air: How stereotypes shape the intellectual identities and performance of women and African-Americans. *American Psy-chologist, 52*, 613–629.

Striblen, C. (2007). Guilt, shame, and shared responsiblity. *Journal of Social Philos-phy, 38*(3), 469–485.

Strossen, N. (2000). *Defending pornography: Free speech, sex, and the fight for women's rights.* New York: New York University Press.

Tangney, J. P., & Dearing, R. L. (2002). *Shame and guilt.* New York: Guilford Press.

Taverner, B., & Montfort, S. (2005). *Making sense of abstinence: Lessons for compre-hensive sex education.* Morristown, NJ: Planned Parenthood of Greater Northern New Jersey.

Thomson, R., & Scott, S. (1991) *Learning about sex: Young women and the social con-struction of identity.* London: Tufnell Press.

Tolman, D. L. (2000). Object lessons: Romance, violence and female adolescent sexual desire. *Journal of Sex Education and Therapy, 25*, 70–79.

Tolman, D. L. (2002). *Dilemmas of desire: Teenage girls talk about sexuality.* Cambridge, MA: Harvard University Press.

Tolman, D. L., & Higgins, T. (1996). How being a good girl can be bad for girls. In N. B. Maglin & D. Perry (Eds.). *Good girls/bad girls: Women, sex, violence and power in the 1990s* (pp. 205–225). New Brunswick, NJ: Rutgers University Press.

Travaglia, L. K., Overall, N. C., & Sibley, C. G. (2009). Benevolent and hostile sex-ism and preferences for romantic partners. *Personality and Individual Differences, 47*, 599–604. doi:10.1016/j.paid.2009.05.015

Trenholm, C., Devaney, B., Fortson, K., Quay, L., Wheeler, J., & Clark, M. (2007). *Impacts of four Title V, Section 510 abstinence education programs: Final report.* Princeton, NJ: Mathematica Policy Research.

Trudell, B. (1992). Inside a ninth-grade sexuality classroom: The process of knowl-edge construction. In J. Sears (Ed.), *Sexuality and the curriculum: The politics and practices of sexuality education* (pp. 203–225). New York: Teachers College.

Trudell, B., & Whatley, M. (1991). Sex Respect: A problematic public school sexu-ality curriculum. *Journal of Sex Education & Therapy, 17*(2), 125–140.

Valenti, J. (2009). *The purity myth: How America's obsession with virginity is hurting young women*. Berkeley, CA: Seal Press.

von Hippel, W., Sekaquaptewa, D., & Vargas, P. (1995). On the role of encoding processes in stereotype maintenance. *Advances in Experimental Social Psychology, 27*, 177–254.

Ward, L. M. (2002). Does television exposure affect emerging adults' attitudes and assumptions about sexual relationships? Correlational and experimental confirmation. *Journal of Youth and Adolescence, 31*, 1–15.

Waxman, H. A.. (2004). *The content of federally funded abstinence-only education programs*. Washington, DC: United States House of Representatives Committee on Government Reform—Minority Staff Special Investigations Division.

Wells, I. B. (1997). Southern horrors: Lynch law in all its phases. In J. J. Royster (Ed.), *Southern horrors and other writings* (pp. 51–61), New York: Bedford Books.

Wertheimer, A. (2003). *Consent to sexual relations*. Cambridge, UK: Cambridge University Press.

Whatley, M. H. (1986). Integrating sexuality issues into the nursing curriculum. *Journal of Sex Education and Therapy, 12*(2), 23–26.

Whatley, M. H. (1987). Biological determinism and gender issues in sexuality education. *Journal of Sex Education and Therapy, 13*(2), 26–29.

Whatley, M. H. (1988). Goals for sex equitable sexuality education. *Peabody Journal of Education, 64*(4), 59–70. doi:10.1080/01619568709538570

Whatley, M. H. (1989). Raging hormones and powerful cars: The construction of men's sexuality in school sex education and popular adolescent films. *Journal of Education, 170*(3), 100–121.

Whatley, M. H. (1999). The "homosexual agenda" goes to school. In D. Epstein & J. Sears (Eds.), *Dangerous knowings: Sexual pedagogies and the master narrative* (pp. 229–241). New York: Cassell.

Whatley, M. H., & Trudell, B. K. (1993). Teen-Aid: Another problematic sexuality curriculum. *Journal Of Sex Education & Therapy, 19*(4), 251–271.

Whorf, B. L. (1940). Science and linguistics. *Technology Review, 42*(6), 229–231, 247–248.

Wiley, D., & Wilson, K. (2009). Just say don't know: Sexuality education in Texas public schools. Retrieved from http://www.tfn.org/site/DocServer/SexEdRort09_web.pdf?docID=981

Wilson, K. L., Goodson, P., Pruitt, B. E., Buhi, E., & Davis-Gunnels, E. (2005). A review of 21 abstinence-only-until-marriage programs. *Journal of School Health, 75*(3), 90–98.

Young, E. W. (1919). Introduction. In N. H. March (Ed.), *Towards racial health: A handbook on the training of boys and girls, parents, teachers and social workers* (pp. xi–xiii). New York: E. P. Dutton & Company.

Young, I. M. (2005). *On female body experience: "Throwing like a girl" and other essays*. Oxford, UK: Oxford University Press.

Young, P. (2002, January). Jessica! The pop temptress unwraps some sexy new moves while saving the big finish for Mr. Right. *Maxim, 49*, 81–89.

Index

About the Author

Sharon Lamb, EdD, is chair and professor in the Department of Counseling and School Psychology in the College of Education and Human Development at the University of Massachusetts Boston. She received her doctoral degree from Harvard University, where she worked with Jerome Kagan and Carol Gilligan. She has published numerous articles on early moral development, sexual development, media and marketing influences on girls' and boys' development, abuse and victimization, and sex education. Her book, *Packaging Girlhood*, co-authored with Lyn Mikel Brown, won a Books for a Better Life Award. Her book, *Sex, Therapy, and Kids: How to Address their Concerns through Talk and Play*, won the book award from the Society for Sex Therapy and Research. She is currently working on a second doctorate in philosophy from the Vrije Universiteit in Amsterdam. Dr. Lamb is also the current president of the Association for Moral Education. Also a licensed psychologist, she has a small therapy practice in Vermont, where she lives with her husband and dog when she is not teaching and doing research.